S.W.A.T. TACTICS

S.W.A.T. TACTICS

BY JEFFRIE JACOBS

PALADIN PRESS
BOULDER, COLORADO

S.W.A.T. Tactics
by Jeffrie Jacobs
Copyright © 1983 by Jeffrie Jacobs

ISBN 0-87364-265-1
Printed in the United States of America

Published by Paladin Press, a division of
Paladin Enterprises, Inc., P.O. Box 1307,
Boulder, Colorado 80306, USA.
(303) 443-7250

Direct inquiries and/or orders to the above address.

Library of Congress Cataloging in Publication Data

Jacobs, Jeffrie.
    S.W.A.T. Tactics

    1. Police—Special weapons and tactics units.
I. Title.   II. Title: SWAT tactics.
HV8080.S64J3 1983   363.2'32   83-6273

Cover photo by John Epperson

Acknowledgments

The author wishes to express thanks and appreciation for the help and cooperation offered by the following organizations and individuals in the preparation of the material contained in this text:

Minds Eye Custom Photography
Photographer Marc Kosa
Project Stream, St. Louis, Missouri
Outdoors Inc., St. Louis, Missouri
Drury Industries
Manager Robert Straeb, Drury Inn, St. Louis
Trio Bowlers Supply, St. Louis, Missouri

The author also gives a special word of thanks to Chief Maurice McCue and to Major Clarence Tiemeyer of the City of St. Ann, Missouri, and to the members of the St. Ann Police Special Weapons and Tactical Team.

Contents

Dedicated to my wife Nancy and to my children Laura and Jeffrie

Introduction

The need for special weapons and tactical teams within small rural and municipal police departments becomes more evident each day. The majority of officers working these less populated geographical areas have been doing so with a false sense of security. When they read about fellow officers being slain during confrontations with barricaded suspects or snipers or in hostage situations, they view these as big-city crime problems. Such confrontations and violent crimes are no longer confined to the big cities. They are spreading to the suburbs and to rural areas at an alarming rate.

Small departments have to deal with limited manpower, low equipment budgets, and the lack of proper training facilities. For these reasons many departments feel that it is inconceivable to develop a special weapons and tactical team. This book has been written to show how a few of these obstacles can be overcome. It will also serve as a guide in the training of a S.W.A.T. team and will outline what action to take in certain tactical situations. By no means is this book an all-inclusive manual; it is designed only to aid the small department in developing a tactical team.

A S.W.A.T. team in training.

1
Organizing the S.W.A.T. Team

The responsibility of a special weapons and tactical (S.W.A.T.) team can be awesome. Therefore, the responsibilities, techniques, and tactics of the team must be set down as guidelines to be followed. Each situation that a team might face will, of course, have its own peculiarities. While the objective is, in general, always the same—to deal with a threatening situation without injury or loss of life to anybody—how this objective can be achieved will necessarily vary. Nevertheless, clearly defined and practiced responsibilities, techniques, and tactics are essential. A disorganized team is a dangerous team—not only to themselves, but to others as well.

The guidelines should be adodpted by the heads of the police department and the controlling government, keeping in mind all other departmental rules and regulations concerning department functions.

PERSONNEL

The first step in developing a S.W.A.T. team is deciding on the team's size and structure. Large departments have assigned up to sixty persons to such a team. They then break these large tactical units down into individual six- or eight-person squads. The squads are spread throughout the city and are scheduled in a manner that allows a 24-hour coverage for tactical assignments.

Smaller departments cannot have the luxury of a tactical unit on duty around-the-clock. The development of one squad consisting of six or eight persons should be adequate for most tactical situations that a small department will encounter. In the accompanying illustration are shown the suggested structures of a six-person team and an eight-person team.

six-person team

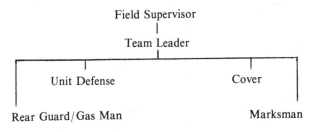

eight-person team

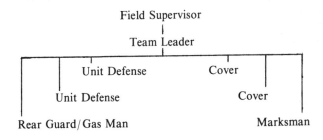

The responsibilities of each team member must be clearly defined. Following is a breakdown of the responsibilities for each of the positions.

Field Supervisor

The field supervisor is responsible for calling out the tactical team and setting up the command post as well as releasing any information given to the press or outside organizations concerning the situation being handled by the team. When to call out the S.W.A.T. team rather than rely on the regular practices of on-duty officers is perhaps the most difficult decision. Normally such situations as an armed and barricaded suspect, armed hostage-taking or kidnapping, or sniper fire are circumstances for S.W.A.T. These incidents are assumed to be S.W.A.T. circumstances in this book, although in some situations involving even these things, the field supervisor might decide otherwise. It should be stressed that a S.W.A.T. team is not the police department's infantry ready to go to "war" with anybody who decides to start throwing rocks at a policeman, nor is it designed for urban guerrilla warfare.

When it is determined that a situation requires S.W.A.T., the field organizer will organize and control the outer perimeter and the staging area, and then solicit special equipment and services as needed by the team. This could include work with such organizations as the gas, electric, phone or water companies, and certainly the fire department and medical services.

Another field supervisor responsibility is the collection of information concerning the situation that might be useful to the team. This information includes specifics regarding the suspect's weapons, hostages (if any), location, and, if possible, the suspect's personality. The field supervisor would immediately pass this information on to the team leader. It would also be the responsibility of the field supervisor to obtain any additional information or equipment requested by the team leader.

Team Leader

The team leader is responsible for the completion of the team's objective. How this is to be done would be dictated by each individual assignment. It is the team leader's responsibility to review the situation and decide what the team's course of action should be.

The team leader must be sure not to limit the team to one course of action on any assignment. It must always be kept in mind that any situation can change, and without an alternate plan of action the team could be caught in the middle of an impossible situation with no planned route of exit. Any circumstance where the team is confronted without a plan of action could cause a loss of credibility with the public as well as with team members, not to mention unnecessarily endangering lives.

The team leader who organizes the procedures to be used when on assignment must keep up to date on all new techniques developed for handling tactical situations. This information should be passed on to the team members during the regular training sessions.

Remember that once on an assignment the team leader is responsible for the action of the team members under his command. This is a grave responsibilite fo one person. For this reason, it is important for all team members to know exactly what their function is to be before the start of any team action. If at any time a team member is unclear regarding his duties, he should inform his leader of this before reaching any assignment position or starting any team action. Only in a life-or-death situation should a team leader accept a team member acting on his own without the knowledge of the team leader. This kind of unit control should not only be adhered to during actual assignments but also during all training sessions. This will prevent team members from being faced with an unfamiliar type of leadership once on assignment.

All communications during any team assignment, as well as information concerning the team's progress, should be given only by the team leader. At no time should any team member be approached by any unauthorized person wishing to obtain information concerning the assignment. Inquiring persons should be directed to the team leader or to the field supervisor.

Cover

The cover will handle the duties as spotter for the team marksman when a marksman's position is chosen. Once the authorization is given for the marksman to fire, the cover pinpoints the target to be fired upon.

The cover is responsible for providing cover fire. This means giving cover fire for advancing team members, assisting the team marksman with anti-sniper fire, and providing intermediate firepower against barricaded suspects to allow the extrication of hostages, innocent bystanders trapped within the kill zone, and any other persons who are vulnerable to injury during the assignment.

Unit Defense

The unit defense provides front-line security and firepower for advancing officers. This team member gives close-range defense against attacks on the team's position. And, when necessary, the unit defense assists the rear guard in delivering chemical agents.

Rear Guard/Gas Man

The rear guard is to provide defense against those suspects who may maneuver to a position that would permit a rear attack on the advancing team. The rear guard provides close-range defense against close-range attacks on the team's position.

It is also the rear guard's duty to collect and preserve all evidence that may be obtained during the assignment. Collecting evidence, however, should not be given priority over the team's immediate objective and certainly never over safety. When collecting evidence, caution should be taken not to endanger the safety of any team member. When necessary, the rear guard is responsible for the use of chemical agents, along with the help of the cover.

Marksman

The marksman is to provide long-range and intermediate-range defense against attacks on advancing team members. The marksman also provides anti-sniper control against long-range weapons fire and provides base-support fire for positioning or advancing team members.

Because of the optical advantage possessed by the marksman's riflescope, it is his responsibility to report any visual change in the suspect's position or any visual, approaching danger to the team. If a situation does not call for the use of a marksman armed with a long-range weapon, the marksman should properly arm himself to assist with the duties and responsibilities of the rear guard/gas man.

The responsibilities of the members of an eight-person team would be the same as that of the six-person team; the only difference is that of two covers and two unit defenses instead of one of each position.

Note that the duties of each team member are listed here in very broad outline form. The responsibilities of these officers cannot be listed in fine detail because their actions may need to change in an instant, usually at the will of the team leader or even that of the suspect being dealt with. Furthermore, if a department adopts a written order concerning the tactical team, and that order details the actions of each team member, the team could lose some of its flexibility. This could hinder the team's ability to react properly to a changing situation.

SELECTING TEAM MEMBERS

After deciding on the size and structure of the department's tactical unit, it must be determined which officers will become members of the team. It is advisable to make a selection of team members from those who volunteer their services for the S.W.A.T. team. One does not feel secure when covered by a person in a firefight in a tactical situation if that person showed no desire to be a team member in the first place.

There are several qualities to keep in mind when considering an officer as a possible candidate for the team. One of these considerations is the officer's mental qualifications and attitudes. An officer should be of average or above-average intelligence. He should show a desire to expand his knowledge concerning his career as a police officer and as a potential team member. He must possess the ability to grasp whatever situation would arise and be able to react quickly while under stress.

The quality important for handling stress is, of course, an emotional one. Emotional stability is essential because members of a tactical unit must possess the ability to handle extreme amounts of stress without losing their ability to think and reason quickly and cearly. Related to this also is the officer's attitude—that it be one of genuine interest in the duties of a police officer.

Beware of officers who react strongly, sometimes violently, toward those who show any argument with their performance or the decisions they make. This type of action may indicate a dangerous sense of insecurity. Any way you wish to describe it, it is a sign of immaturity. A tactical team is no place to assign an officer who cannot control his emotions.

The last, but not the least significant quality to look for in a possible candidate is an officer's physical qualifications. An officer should not be checking his physical condition just for the reason of becoming a member of the tactical team. Any officer who all along has failed to keep himself in good physical condition shows a lack of concern for his own ability to perform his duties as a police officer.

However, recognizing that a majority of today's police officers may have fallen below those physical standards achieved in their training facility when first hired by the department, improved physical condition may have to be acquired once the team is selected. All candidates must be made aware that all team members will be required to be in top physical condition and that if this is not achieved, they will not be considered for a position as a team member. Actually and ideally, it is not only important for tactical team members to be in top physical condition, but all members of the department should strive for this goal.

Individual equipment listed on page five.

2

Equipment

A professional S.W.A.T. team must be equipped with top quality equipment. The words "top quality" do not mean going out to the local retail police equipment establishment and loading the team down with an assortment of overpriced, impractical items that would be more trouble than they are worth. The team should be equipped with good but practical equipment.

Each officer assigned to a special weapons and tactical team is required to carry special equipment. All the items contained in the individual equipment list that follows are not mandatory for a team to function, but once the team begins its training, it will become apparent which items are needed and that the use of them may save the lives of team members, as well as enable the team to accomplish its objective with more efficiency.

INDIVIDUAL EQUIPMENT

uniform*
ballistic vest*
handgun and holster*
knife (boot type)

ammunition
pencil and note pad
poncho (rain type)
first-aid kit*
mirror with telescopic handle
flexcuffs
length of rope (⅛-inch nylon)
tape (black electrical)
wrist watch
assigned weapon*
wood wedge
flashlight
swiss seat
carabiner
gloves

* Item will be discussed in the choice of equipment section that follows.

Besides individual equipment, each team needs a certain amount of specialized equipment. All the equipment listed here will not be needed in every situation the team might be called on to handle, but each item has its use by tactical teams at one time or another.

5

TEAM EQUIPMENT

chemical agents*
gas masks
hand-held radios
binoculars
flares
first-aid trauma kit*
grappling hook and rope*
ammunition box and extra ammunition*
tool kit containing miscellaneous tools*
bullhorn
fire extinguisher
riot helmets and gas launchers
200 feet ⅜-inch nylon rope

*Item will be discussed in the choice of equipment section that follows.

Most items are small enough to be carried in hand-held equipment bags. This keeps all equipment portable enough to be carried to the assignment location without the need of a special vehicle. Also, the equipment can be carried by team members when on assignment without a great deal of trouble.

CHOOSING TEAM EQUIPMENT

The choice of many items is cut-and-dried. One example is *nylon* rope instead of other types because of its durability, strength, and rot-proof quality. The availability of telescopic mirrors and electrical tape at most auto parts stores makes the gathering of this equipment easy. Some items may be acquired by having team members check their homes and garages for materials to put into the team toolbox.

The following illustration shows an average tool kit that can be carried and used by a small department's tactical team, and all the items shown are easily obtained.

The soft carrying case makes the tool kit portable enough for the team to carry the kit while handling a tactical situation.

The team trauma kit should contain supplies to maintain first-aid treatment until proper medical attention can be obtained. It is important to realize that during a tactical situation a person may become injured, and proper medical attention may not be available for some time. For this reason this kit contains supplies for fractures of bones, serious bleeding, and other traumas.

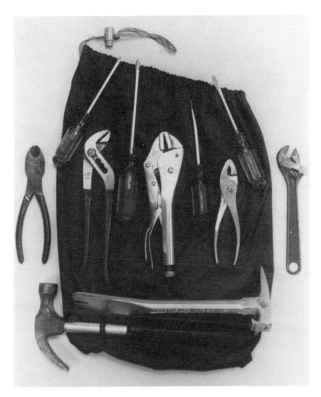

Tool kit.

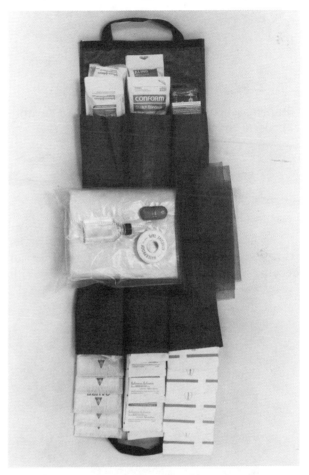

The first-aid kit carried by each team member should contain what is needed to handle most wounds for a short period of time.

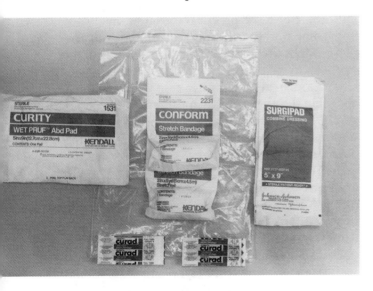

The trauma kit contains: (1) abdominal wet-proof pads, (2) trauma pads, (3) snakebite kit, (4) disposable emergency blanket, (5) wire splint material, (6) tape, (7) plastic container of distilled water, (8) ice pack, (9) tongue-press sticks, (10) triangle bandage, (11) 4-inch and 2-inch gauze pads, and (12) small sheet of plastic.

There may be other items that a team would wish to put into such a trauma kit for their own particular needs. It is important, though, to keep this kit as portable as possible.

First-aid supplies also come in individual containers for compact storage. This is also a good way to transport the supplies. These

The kit shown contains: (1) abdominal wet proof pad, (2) trauma pad, (3) two rolls 2-inch gauze, and (4) two band-aids. All of these items are contained in a plastic bag, which can assist in treating a chest wound.

complete sets of first-aid supplies tend to be more expensive than assembling one's own kit.

UNIFORMS

The uniform of the tactical team should differ from the regular duty uniform. Dark blue has become a preferred color for tactical units. This

dark color allows for blending with shadows and nighttime darkness for concealment. Several departments use a two-piece navy blue work uniform. For more practical purposes, many are now going to the jump-suit type of uniform. The jump-suit uniform can be put on over other clothing to save time in changing clothes. This also means greater warmth in cold weather. When choosing the uniform, one must remember not to choose a uniform that is equipped with shiny buttons or metal snaps that would shine in the dark or reflect light. There should be a department patch or insignia on each sleeve of the uniform, but no badges should be worn on the front. A baseball-type cap is used for head gear; this hat allows for comfort and will shade the eyes from the sun.

Ballistics equipment is as essential for a tactical team as the weapons they carry. There are several considerations to keep in mind when choosing ballistics equipment. One is what protection level one desires. Some equipment will only protect against small caliber handgun ammunition, whereas other material will stop everything up to and including a high-powered, armor-piercing (a.p.) rifle round. The most comfortable type of vest now being used by many departments is the well-known, soft-body armor. This can be purchased in a variety of colors, sizes, and shapes. It is lightweight and can be purchased to wrap around the upper torso for complete upper-torso protection. Soft-body armor is available for protection against all handgun ammunition up to and including the .44 magnum (a.p. ammo not included). Soft-body armor can be equipped with hard ballistic panels to raise its protection levels against the higher caliber weapons.

Hard-body armor can be purchased that will defeat most pistol and rifle ammunition. When using hard-body armor, some mobility and comfort are sacrificed; the hard-body armor weighs much more than the soft-body armor.

When choosing armor for the team, don't fall for fancy name advertising or be swayed by fancy designs. Many ballistics equipment companies offer a tactical vest with numerous attractive features, such as pockets for carrying tactical equipment. The main drawback with this type of equipment is the extra price one must pay for such features.

Pictured here is a lightweight, soft-body vest that has had pockets added to it by team members after this less expensive armor was purchased.

This also allows for constructing the vest according to one's own specifications. Also pictured are the high level ballistic inserts.

WEAPONS

Each team member is equipped with two weapons. One is the handgun, and the other is the assigned team weapon. The handgun is primarily designed as a back-up gun but is resorted to in tight locations where a long gun is impractical. There are only two types of handguns that should be considered for this type of work; one is the double-action revolver and the other is the auto-loader. The choice between the two should be easy. If the officers of the department are already familiar with and are now carrying a double-action revolver, that is the handgun they should use on the team. Likewise, those carrying auto-loading handguns should use their familiar weapons.

For a tactical team, carrying a handgun in a shoulder holster is the most desirable way to carry the weapon. A shoulder holster helps keep the weapon out of the way when maneuvering with

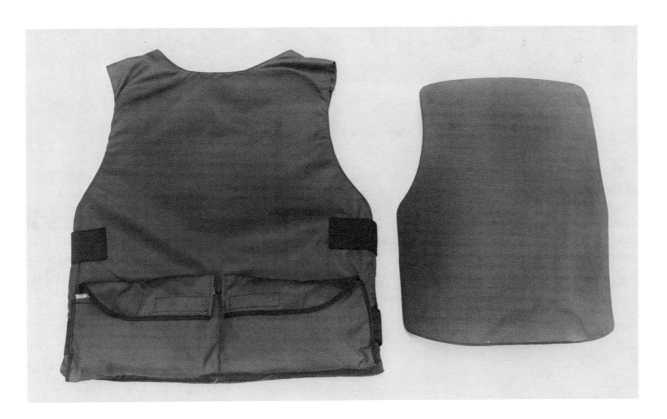

the assigned-team, long weapon. The shoulder holster also avoids the need for wearing a belt if the team is using the jump-suit as a team uniform.

Assigned Weapons

Volumes could be written on the different styles and calibers of weapons available for a tactical team. For the sake of simplicity, I have broken this choice down in to what seems to be the most popular and widely used weapons by tactical teams at this time.

Shotgun with sling. Keep in mind the many uses that the shotgun may be called upon to perform. Its primary function is close-range support fire, but this weapon may also be used for delivering chemical agents or for providing distant cover fire with the use of rifle slugs. One may at times need to attach a chemical launcher to the barrel of this weapon.

support and anti-sniper control. The four most commonly used weapons chosen for this type of work are the .30-caliber carbine (M1), Mini-14, M-16, and AR 15 .223-caliber rifles. Any one of the four would be a good choice because of their effective range, accuracy, and availability. All four are fairly simple to operate and maintain. If one desires another weapon besides these, the factors of range, accuracy, and availability should be kept in mind while making the choice.

I would suggest not using a fully automatic or machinegun-type rifle for this task. It is too easy to fire more rounds than necessary, and weapons control is a must for a tactical team.

Anti-sniper rifle with sling. The caliber most commonly used for anti-sniper control is 30'06-.308 or .223. These calibers provide long-distance accuracy and substantial force upon impact. The bolt action is chosen for the officer to concentrate on the "One-Shot Effect." Any indiscriminate firing by an officer, especially with this type of

Twelve-gauge pump shotgun with folding stock and extended tube.

The most popular type of shotgun now being chosen is the 12-gauge pump that is equipped with a front-bead sight and a folding stock. The folding stock accommodates maneuverability in tight quarters, and an extended tube can be added for more firepower without the need for reloading.

Assault rifle (semiautomatic with sling). One of the most controversial issues that faces a tactical team today is what to choose for close-range

long-range weapon, is strictly forbidden. This rifle should be equipped with at least a 3 × 9, variable telescopic sight with a post and cross hair, inverted post, or four-tapered post reticle. A heavy barrel would help cut down on recoil. It is also necessary that this weapon be equipped with a sling to aid in transporting the weapon and to help steady the rifle when fired.

From top to bottom: .30-caliber M-1 Carbine (semi-auto), .223-caliber Ruger Mini-14 (semi-auto), .223-caliber Colt AR-15 (semi-auto), .223-caliber Colt M-16 (semi-/full auto).

From top to bottom: .30'06-caliber Mauser (modified-bolt action), .308-caliber Remington model 700ADL (bolt action), .223-caliber Remington model 700 BDL (bolt action).

3
Training

Once it has been determined which officers are going to make up the team and a certain amount of the team's equipment has been assembled, a training schedule has to be set up. The training schedule must be one that is attended by all team members. This is especially important so that all members will become aware of each other's abilities and can learn how to work as a team.

Needless to say, for a small department there may not be many times when the entire team can gather together for training. A training day should be set aside for one day a month and scheduled far enough in advance that other officers of the department can fill in where the manpower may be cut short during regular duty.

These training days should consist of a regular eight-hour training program, in which all areas of the training can be performed. Other training schedules can be established at various times through the rest of the month; these two- or three-hour sessions can include those portions of the training that do not require the presence of all the team members or that are "classroom" in nature.

Never set a goal for the completion of the training. A tactical team should and will never finish its training. There are always new ideas and methods to practice in handling tactical situations, and there will always be room for improvement.

PHYSICAL CONDITIONING

One of the most important segments of the team's training, and probably the most frustrating, is the team's physical fitness. All team members must adhere to a strict physical fitness program. This type of program should be practiced on the officers' own time as well as during team training sessions. The following exercise routine has been developed to accommodate team members in the area of muscle development and proper stretching to help prevent strained muscles and tendons during training or team functions.

Start with the warm-up exercise and work through in the order as listed.

1. Warm-up stretching

With legs spread, cross your arms at the chest and bend to the front; straighten up and then bend to each side. Keep the knees locked straight. If done properly, a burning sensation should be felt behind the knees.

2. Wide-hand pushups

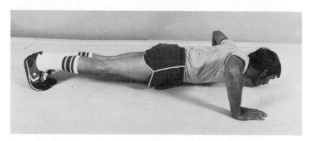

Perform the same motion as a regular pushup, except for placing your hands more widely apart than normal. This will work the full range of chest muscles while expanding and stretching the rib cage.

3. Sit-ups

Bending the knees helps to develop the upper and mid-range abdominal muscles. Fingers should be kept locked behind the head. When maximum height is reached, grunt and exhale all air while concentrating on tightening the lower abdominal muscles.

4. Front-leg raises

Stand in a walking position with one leg in front of the other. Keeping the rear knee locked, kick the rear leg forward and up. Then return the leg to its original position. Ten repetitions per leg per workout is sufficient. A burning sensation should be felt behind the knee.

5. Side-leg raise

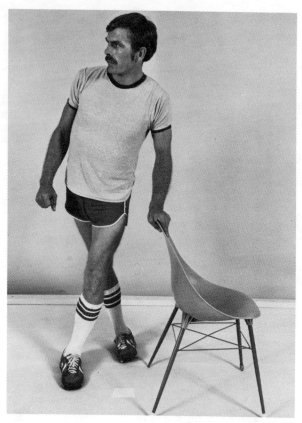

Use a chair or other object for balance, and stand with one leg crossed behind the other. Keeping the rear knee straight, swing the rear leg out. This will cause a burning sensation in the groin and hip area if performed properly.

6. Tricep press

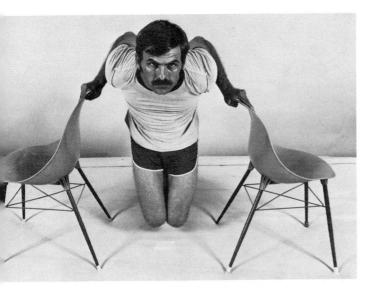

This exercise works that portion of the arm that will develop the fastest but is usually the least worked. The use of two chairs will allow for a full extension. Lower yourself as far as possible.

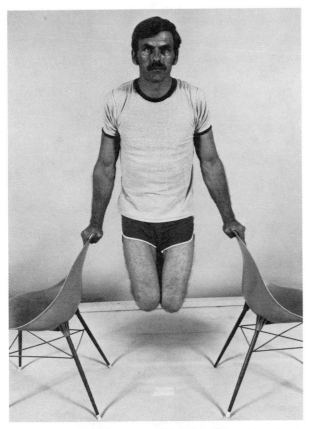

Keeping your elbows tucked in will concentrate this exercise to the desired muscle group. Upon rising, concentrate on a full extension.

When one has not been exercising or working out for some time, soreness and stiffness can be expected after a workout. Sticking to an exercise or workout schedule three or four times a week for several weeks is the only way to overcome this.

Contrary to popular belief, an exercise program can serve the purpose of weight loss or gain. How the exercise is performed determines whether one loses or gains weight. The most favorable point about gaining weight through exercise is that the weight gain will be lean muscle weight instead of the unwanted water or fat weight.

Using these exercises to lose weight can be accomplished by going through the repetitions with speed. To accomplish the goal of gaining weight, perform the exercises slowly—similar to isometric exercising. The use of weight-lifting equipment, if available, will cause weight gain or loss at a faster rate than exercises. Unfortunately, weight-lifting equipment is not always available to all departments.

That an exercise program can help with weight control does not mean you can overlook the importance of proper diet and amount of sleep. Working out for twenty minutes, then eating a dinner that would satisfy two people, then going to bed and sleeping for ten hours is not using good judgment. Going in the opposite direction—skipping dinner and getting just three or four hours of sleep—will only compound physical problems. Diet and sleep should be put on a schedule along with the workout program and should be adhered to.

FALLING AND ROLLING

Officers dealing with tactical situations may find themselves forcibly disarming suspects, defending themselves from attack, and undertaking physical feats not usually faced by regular duty officers. For this reason all team members must not only be aware of, but must be able to perform several tumbling exercises—falling, diving, and rolling. The following techniques have been designed to teach officers how to fall forward and backward with the ability to avoid injury. Also covered is the technique that allows an officer to move over low to chest-high objects with the greatest amount of speed and the least amount of exposure.

Prior to each training session in this area, the exercises and stretching routine should be performed to prevent unnecessary injuries. The following techniques should also be practiced on tumbling mats, soft ground, or heavy carpet. Practicing these techniques on a hard surface may cause injury to the wrist, knees, elbows, or shoulder joints. Notice that in all of the falling techniques, the fingers are spread and the same surface is used for landing, whether it is with one hand or two. The impact of the fall should be absorbed by the entire surface from the elbow to the fingertips.

Another helpful tip, to avoid being winded when falling, is to exhale upon reaching the ground. One does this by yelling, forcing all the air out of the lungs and tightening the stomach muscles at the same time contact is made with the ground. This makes landing less painful due to an increase in the flow of adrenalin. It also prevents the possibility of your breath being knocked out upon impact.

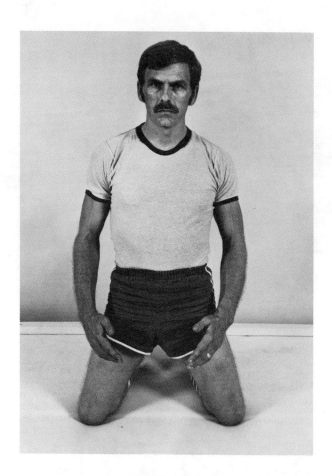

Front Fall

Begin learning the front fall from the kneeling position. Bending at the waist, rotate the arms with the hands spread, and bring them down hard on the mat. It is very important that the entire surface from the elbow to the fingertips strike the mat at the same time. If the elbow strikes first or if just the hands are used, the result will be pain and possible injury.

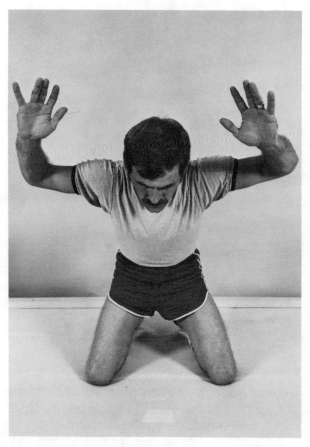

Try keeping the arms at a 90-degree angle when striking the mat, and get into the habit of turning your face to the left. This will prevent objects such as broken glass or branches on the ground from hitting you in the eyes and face.

Wrong

Wrong

After performing the front fall from the kneeling position, move on to the front fall from a standing position. With your legs spread, again bend at the waist and drive the upper part of the body toward the mat using the same striking technique as before.

Next, attempt to master the front fall from a standing position in the following manner. With feet one shoulder-width apart, throw the feet back with a small hop, and fall forward. The motion should be stopped using the same striking technique as before.

Notice that the fallen person (see photograph) landed with his legs spread and is up on his toes. He also has his head turned to the side to prevent face injuries.

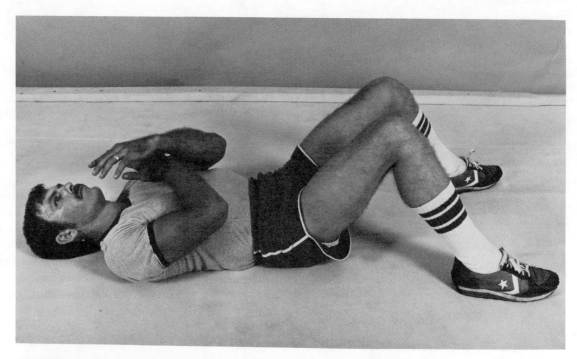

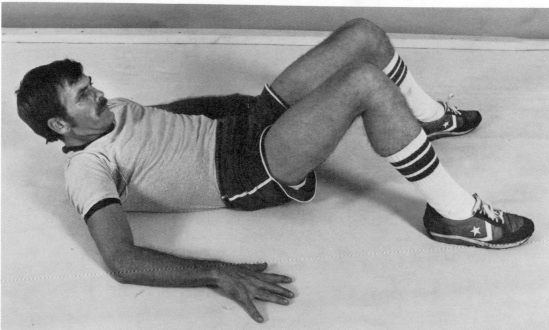

Back Fall

The back fall is one of the most difficult techniques to perform because of the built-in fear of blindly falling backwards. One thing important to remember when executing a back fall is where you have been. Always remember what is lying directly behind you.

Begin practicing the back fall by lying on your back and crossing the arms over the chest with the fingers spread. Then bring both arms down fast and hard, striking the mat close to the body. The mat must be struck with both arms at the same time. When striking the mat, use the same surface of the arm as with the front fall. Use enough force striking down to cause your head to lift from the mat. As fast as the mat is struck, the arms should be returned to their crossed position and the head lowered to the mat. This technique should be practiced until the weight of the body is felt being lifted off the mat by the force of the downward strike.

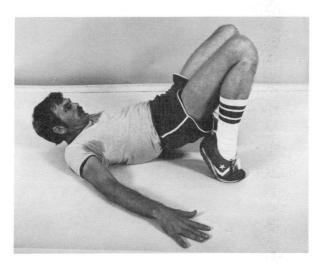

Once the mat is being struck with enough force, move on to practicing the back fall from a squatting position. Arch the back and fall back using the same striking technique to break the fall. The arms should hit the mat an instant before the body. If the mat is struck with enough force, the force of the fall should not be felt.

This should be practiced until the timing and striking power are perfectly coordinated. Do not move on to the final step until this has been accomplished.

The final step is to perform the back fall from a semi-squat position. Fall back, kicking the feet out in front. Use the same striking technique as before to break the fall.

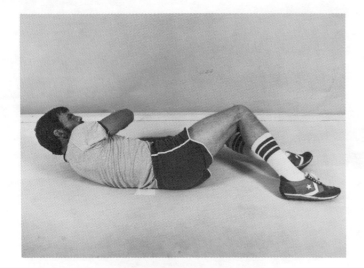

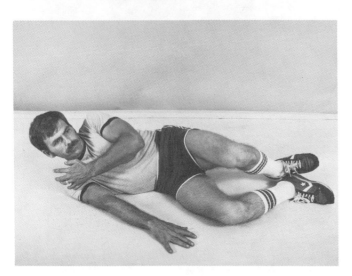

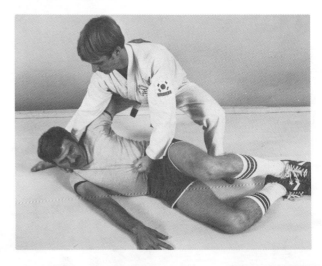

Side Fall

The side fall is a difficult technique to practice, except in the actual motion of being taken down by an opponent. This is a defense motion which allows one to take the shock of a fall away from the hip and shoulder and to absorb the shock with the free arm.

Practice by lying on your back and rolling from side to side, striking the mat with the arm closest to the mat. Strike with enough force to stop the rolling motion. When the mat is struck with enough force, the hip and shoulder can be felt lifting from the mat.

Graduating to a slow hip toss will help you practice the side fall while at the same time learning the fundamentals of the judo hip-toss technique.

Forward Roll

This technique is most helpful when an officer is carrying a long gun and is shoved from behind or trips over something and finds himself falling forward but, because of the long gun, cannot apply the front falling technique.

The first surface to contact the ground is the arm and shoulder. This is accomplished by dipping one shoulder to the ground and rolling on the upper arm and shoulder, keeping the head to one side. Once the rolling motion is begun, curl the back and legs and continue rolling until the forward position is resumed.

In order to prevent injury from falling on a hard object, a padded broom handle can be used as a training aid. This roll and all techniques in this section should never be practiced with department weapons. **At no time should any hand-to-hand or tumbling practice be done with any type of loaded weapon!**

rump. Maintaining the rear motion, curl the back and let the legs roll over the top of the head. Finish by leaning to one shoulder, keeping the head to the side. Once over the shoulder, push up with both arms and maintain balance with the feet.

Back Roll

The back roll is performed in a similar manner to the front roll, the difference being that the motion is to the rear. While falling backward, bend the legs and take the brunt of the fall on the

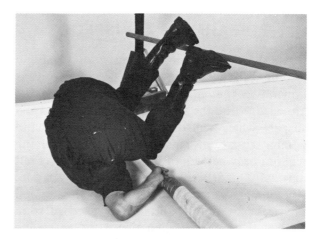

Forward Diving Roll

The forward diving roll is a technique that can be used to move with speed over objects waist high to chest high, and with a minumum of exposure to a possible suspect.

This is performed the same as the forward roll, except that one dives into the forward roll position. To start the practice, begin with a very low position and move up to the higher positions.

This may seem like a rather extreme way to travel over low objects, when you could just as easily jump over the object and stay on your feet. Keep in mind that when moving over an object in an upright position, the entire body is exposed, making a much larger target. If a team member is ever advancing on a position and gets caught under fire, this technique can be very effective in moving out of the line of fire.

DISARMING A SUSPECT

Along with the small number of tumbling techniques that have been described, it is imperative that all team members possess the knowledge and the ability to physically disarm a suspect when confronted with a hand-to-hand combat situation. This knowledge and training will not only help an officer disarm a suspect but may assist an officer in retaining his own weapon. (By the way, officers who feel that being in good physical condition is of little importance will soon change their minds when they start practicing these hand-to-hand combat techniques.)

When an officer is faced with the task of defending himself in a hand-to-hand combat situation, it is important for him to know *where* and *where not* to strike a person. It would be a very disheartening thing for an officer to strike an assailant with a devastating punch just to have the assailant stand and look at the officer as if nothing had happened. And this happens. One warning, however, with regard to practicing these techniques with the other members of the team: Be careful. Keep your distance and practice using controlled striking, much as is done in the martial arts.

The areas to strike for the maximum effect are designated in the following diagram (Diagram Number 1), as empty circles (O). These are the areas that, when struck with enough force, can stop an assailant with nonfatal injuries. Some of these areas may cause broken bones or a temporary paralysis of that area, but this should not keep you from using these techniques, because most paralysis will pass in a short period of time, and a broken bone can be medically attended to once the suspect is in custody. The areas marked with a solid circle (•) designate areas that, when struck with enough force, could be fatal. These areas should be used only as a last resort.

STRIKING POINTS

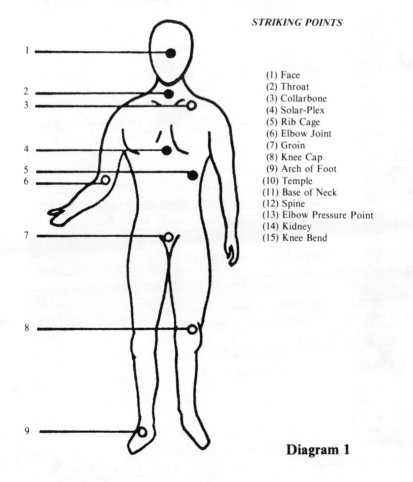

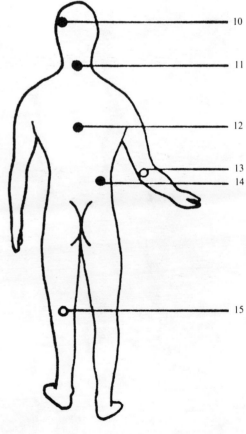

(1) Face
(2) Throat
(3) Collarbone
(4) Solar-Plex
(5) Rib Cage
(6) Elbow Joint
(7) Groin
(8) Knee Cap
(9) Arch of Foot
(10) Temple
(11) Base of Neck
(12) Spine
(13) Elbow Pressure Point
(14) Kidney
(15) Knee Bend

Diagram 1

All of these areas should be kept in mind when practicing any defensive hand-to-hand combat techniques, so that when faced with a combat situation, these moves will become reflex actions. It is important not to have to stop and think about where to strike a suspect. Any time an officer must take to think during a combat situation may be enough time for the suspect to make a move that could be disabling or even fatal to the officer.

Covered in this section is the disarming of suspects who are armed with a rifle and/or handgun. There are many writings that describe numerous ways to defend oneself in such situations. The techniques described here have been developed with the notion that an officer of a S.W.A.T. team will probably be restricted by tactical equipment, and that movement, therefore, will be somewhat impaired.

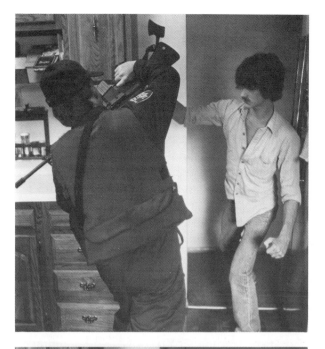

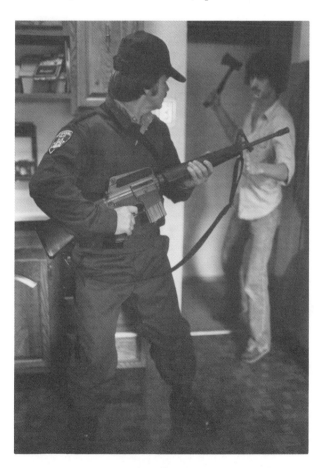

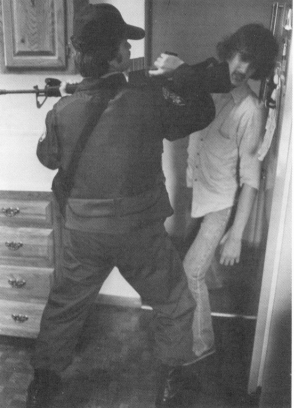

Regardless if attacked from the rear or from the front, you must react instantly. The first reaction of the officer should be to block or redirect the weapon directed at him, away from him. If the officer is armed with a long gun, this should be used as the blocking instrument.

A sweeping motion should be used with the long gun, and as soon as the block is made, a return striking blow should be made to incapacitate the assailant. But never strike or block with the barrel of a weapon; this can damage the gun. Use the stock or butt of the weapon. (If the blocking motion has knocked the weapon from the assailant's grasp, a less damaging method may be used to subdue him.)

Remember that the objective is to subdue the suspect with only the amount of force necessary. The blocking motion alone may cause enough surprise to allow you to step away from the suspect and hold him at bay, with a weapon, while other officers take him into custody. If this should occur, the cover should move in quickly, not giving the suspect time to regain his thoughts and to launch a physical attack on the first officer's position. Also be sure that when the cover moves in to take the suspect into custody, none of the cover's weapons are within reach of the suspect.

In the event that an officer falls hostage to an armed assailant, there are several techniques that can be used. These techniques have been designed to disarm a suspect once he has allowed himself to come within arm's reach. You must keep in mind that these techniques are only to be attempted when there are no other persons, such as other hostages, whose safety may be at stake. Also, these techniques should not be tried unless you have the confidence that the technique can be applied properly and that you are physically able to complete the technique.

The situation most likely to be encountered is where you are held at gunpoint with a handgun. If the assailant keeps a safe distance away and is aware of every move, any action on the part of an officer would be foolish. Going along with the assailant's wishes and cooperating may cause him to relax and drop his guard. This may bring him closer, which would give you the opportunity to make a move.

The first motion is to change the direction in which the gun is pointed, and without hesitation take whatever action is needed to overcome the assailant. This will probably be a blow to a vital spot and a take-down technique that will incapacitate him.

When face to face with an armed suspect, an officer should never try to raise his hands above his head. The elbows should be kept close to the body. This is necessary for the following moves.

Forcing the gun to the outside would enable the gunman to bend his wrist and continue to point the gun at the officer. Also, most average persons have more strength to pull their arms in toward their bodies than to push their arms back across the front of their bodies.

When faced with a suspect with a handgun, any action must be quick and forceful. The handgun and arm should be forced across the front of the gunman's body. Then his wrist or the weapon itself should be grasped and held tightly.

As quickly as the gun is forced across the body, a slight step should be taken into the assailant. A strong fist strike is delivered to his groin or abdomen, reaching, of course, under the blocking arm. Take notice that the first step is with the foot on the same side as the blocking arm.

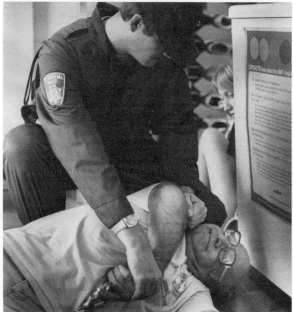

After the first strike, continue the forward motion while taking hold of the assailant's gun arm with both hands; with the other leg, step slightly past the assailant. Once in this position, twist the body and force the suspect over the forward leg and down hard to the ground.

Once the suspect is on the ground, deliver a hard knee drop to the side of the neck or the head. At this point, his resistance should subside.

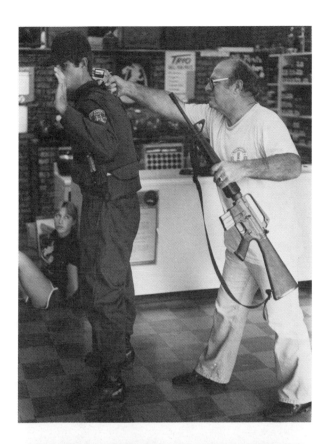

A rear-gun attack is handled in the same basic manner as a face-to-face encounter with just a small deviation. First it must be determined in which hand the assailant is holding the gun.

Notice that the officer's hands are being held with the elbows close to his side (see photograph). Just a quick peek will let him know which hand holds the gun.

Once this is determined, the upper portion of the body can be turned and the gun again blocked across the body of the assailant. As quickly as the gun is blocked, the foot on the blocking side is slid toward the assailant, and a hard strike delivered to the side of his head or neck. During this striking motion, control of the gun arm should be maintained with the blocking hand.

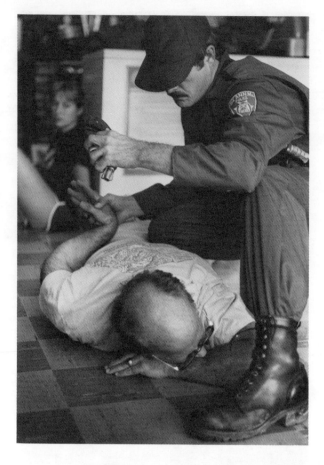

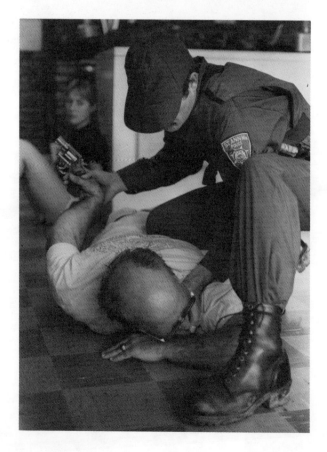

After delivering the striking blow, reach around the assailant's head and take hold of his chin, hair, or anything that can be taken hold of, and twist his head around by pulling with both arms. Pull him to the ground in front, maintaining control of the gun arm all the time. The twist of your own body will give the necessary leverage.

As with the first technique, drop down hard with a knee strike to the side of the assailant's head or neck. At this point take control of the gun and take the suspect into custody.

 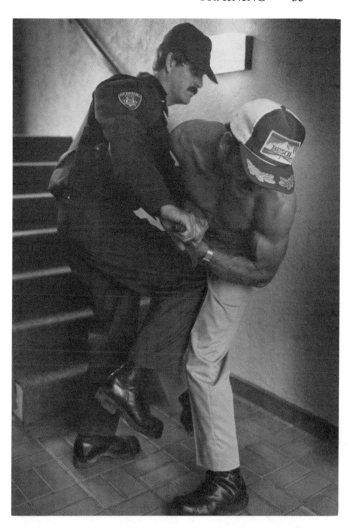

A person armed with a rifle or shotgun does not have to be as close to you for you to take action to disarm him. When face to face with a man with a rifle, the first action is similar to the handgun technique. First block the gun across the front of his body, but use both hands while stepping forward and delivering a knee strike to the assailant's groin or abdomen.

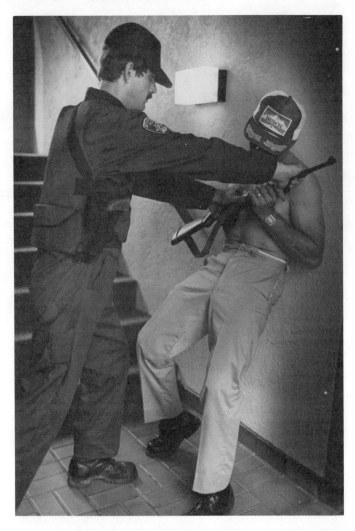 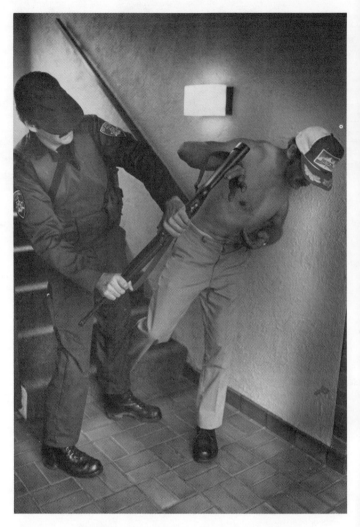

Continue the forward motion, driving the assailant back while grasping the butt of the gun. With a good grasp on the weapon, push the weapon into the suspect and then pull it away hard, twisting the body while stepping away. This action will either remove the weapon from his grasp or throw him to the ground in front of you. If the weapon is taken from his grasp, twist back, striking the assailant with the butt of the weapon, or quickly step away, removing the weapon from his reach.

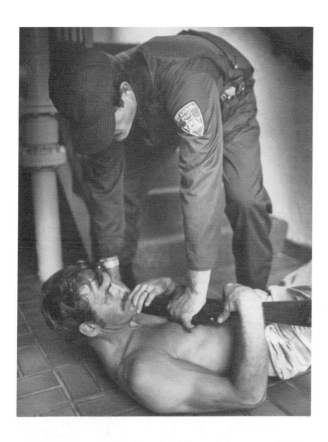

If the assailant is thrown to the ground and does not lose grasp of the weapon, using your own body weight, the weapon should be driven into the chest or face of the assailant. Again, stepping back and twisting the weapon should remove it from his grasp.

Using a foot against his chin or neck for leverage to pull the gun from his grasp may help and might even be necessary against a particularly strong assailant.

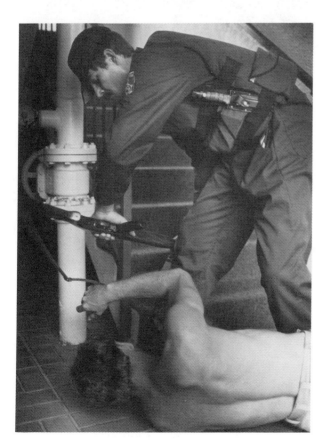

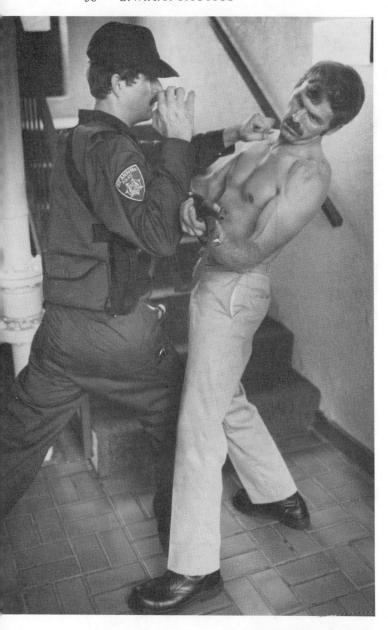

efficient manner. Most officers who have a little time in on the street have made arrests, and once the situation seemed to be under control, they may have let their guard down and begun to relax. This is not something that any training officer would like to hear, but in certain given situations one may get away with this sort of arrest control. When dealing with a tactical situation, one is dealing with a suspect who has taken his challenge to law enforcement to the maximum. Because of this, I do not feel there is any room for relaxation.

There are a considerable number of handcuffing styles as well as proper pat down and searching techniques. Many of these are correct for certain arrests, such as traffic warrants and the like, although one must always maintain control and be on guard. In the tactical situation, once a suspect is taken into custody, he should be dealt with by two officers, or more if required, to properly control his actions.

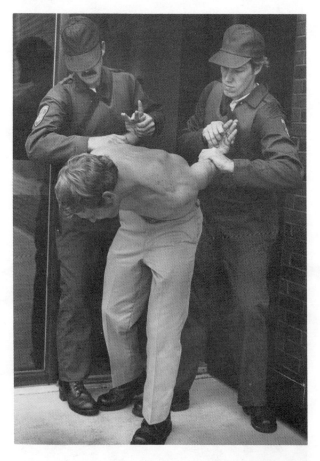

When faced from the rear with a long gun, again turn and block the gun across the assailant's body, delivering a hard fist strike to the neck or head of the assailant.

Then turn and grasp the gun as in the front technique and continue the disarming motion with the proper twist and pulling as previously described.

These actions have to be performed with great speed and force in order to work properly. It must be stressed again that these techniques should be undertaken as a last resort, and that care must be taken not to endanger the lives of other hostages.

Taking a suspect into custody and the final arrest also need to be accomplished in a safe and

Both arms and wrists should be held and controlled until the suspect has been led away from the area or building he occupied. This may call for leading the suspect out of a building and into the open, such as the front yard of a house or

FIREARMS TRAINING

a sidewalk in front of a business. There is no problem with any of these locations so long as they are within the inner perimeter. To search the suspect, he should be laid face down with one officer controlling his actions while the other officer conducts the search. If the suspect is lying face down with arms and feet spread, he will have little chance to take action against anybody.

Once it is determined that he is free of weapons from the rear, his arms should be handcuffed behind him, and he should be rolled over to finish the search.

After he has been neutralized, he should be taken out of the area. The area should then be secured for the crime-scene investigator, and you should begin your own final report investigation of the crime scene.

It would be to the benefit of the firearms instructor as well as the team members for the instructor to go back to the basics when beginning firearms training. Some of the members may feel that this is not necessary. The best way to explain beginning from the initial gun familiarization class is that it is the only way all team members can know for certain that the other team members are sure of what they are doing when handling firearms. I have never seen any of this training wasted, and a refresher course on weapons handling, cleaning, and control can only improve a team's knowledge of the weapons they will use in life-and-death situations.

All officers must be qualified with all the team's weapons. Their qualification should be above that normally required of duty officers. Not all members will have the same ability, but all should have an expert rating.

Each individual officer's performance must be kept in mind when deciding which officer will fill which position on the team. An officer who consistently scores a 99 percent with the high-powered rifle would be assigned the sniper or marksman position over that of another officer who scores only in the 80s.

Training team members with firearms begins in the classroom. Several classes should be held, familiarizing the team with the working and cleaning of team weapons. Each department will have to set its own policy on firearms control, keeping within all state and local laws.

Training officers with the use of team weapons is easiest by starting at short distances and progressing to the greater distances. When using long-range weapons, there are bullet and weapon characteristics one must know.

It may be found that the high-powered rifle, such as the 30'06 or the .308-caliber rifle, is hard to fire in rapid succession with pinpoint accuracy. This may be due to surprise at the weapon's recoil. It may also be caused by the tuning fork effect of the barrel when fired. Whatever the reason, scoring more consistently may be achieved by waiting several seconds between shots to allow time for these problems to subside.

Duty ammunition should be used in all practice sessions at the firing range. There is a big difference in some types of ammunition. If team members are using .38 wad-cutters at the range

and carry .357 Mag. ammo when on assignment, the greater recoil of the magnum ammunition may cause a short surprise delay before firing another round. That short amount of delay could cost someone his life.

The most common type of firearms practice now being used by police departments is the stationary target time fire. This is good training for weapon familiarization but affords the officer no opportunity to decide for himself when or when not to fire. Good guy, pop-up targets are very popular for the decision-making type of training. There are several companies that offer electronic or hydraulic target systems. The pop-up targets being used in the following photographs are homemade spring-activated targets designed by members of the St. Ann, Missouri, Police S.W.A.T. team and are now being used by the entire department.

A 50-yard firing range can be used for training with the pistol, assault rifles, and shotguns. The range should include objects for the officers to use as cover and concealment training. Portable pop-up targets should be placed in locations that will give officers practice firing at different angles.

When team members go through their training, it should be as if on assignment. Two officers going through at the same time will assist in teaching the officers the techniques of cover and support fire. Extreme caution and strict obedience of all safety rules is a must in this type of training. Long-range weapon fire with the assault rifle and sniper rifle must be practiced at a range or an area that will afford at least a 300-yard firing practice.

All team members must be familiar with the trajectory of the ammunition they are using (see Diagram Number 2) to properly determine the correct aiming point discussed later in this chapter.

The most difficult shooting that the team marksman may encounter is a moving target, especially at ranges beyond 200 yards. The greater the distance between the shooter and the target, the more difficult it is to judge the speed and angle

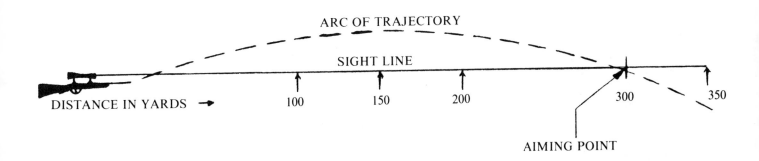

Diagram 2

LEADS

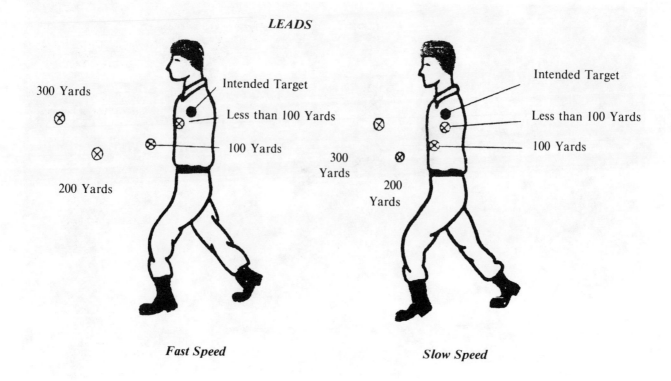

Fast Speed   *Slow Speed*

The solid black circle indicates the intended point of impact for all shots. The circle containing the X indicates the aiming point for the given distance, depending on the suspect's speed, for a hit at the intended point of impact. . . .

Diagram 3

of the target. The marksman will have to aim far enough in front of the moving target so the target and the bullet will meet. This distance between the target and the aiming point is called the "lead." For practical purposes, shown in Diagram Number 3 is an example of the lead in two different situations. One situation is a person who is moving in a slow, cautious manner, and another is a person who is traveling at a double-time running speed.

Engaging laterally moving targets at ranges of up to 200 yards, the marksman must lead the target about 4 inches forward of the intended point of impact. Therefore, holding a bead on the forward edge of the abdomen will inflict a serious wound in the body area. At 400 yards, the shooter must use a lead of approximately 15 inches. Again this will depend on the speed of the target and, of course, the weapon being used.

It has been determined that the lead must be decreased when a target is moving from left to

right across the range of a right-handed shooter. This is probably due to the difficulty for a right-handed shooter to completely follow through on his shots. He has a tendency to pause just as he shoots, allowing the target to move in front of the shot. The opposite would be true for a left-handed shooter. For targets moving at an angle toward or away from the marksman, the lead is reduced to 70 percent of that necessary for those moving at a 90-degree angle.

It is not practical for a marksman to shoot at a moving target beyond 500 yards. At these distances it becomes a hit-and-miss situation, and the target becomes smaller than the margin of error in range estimation, speed estimation, and angle estimation.

The marksman not only has to deal with leads in moving targets, but he also has to contend with the rise and drop of the bullet when target distance changes, without resighting the weapon. If the department's scoped weapon is sighted-in at

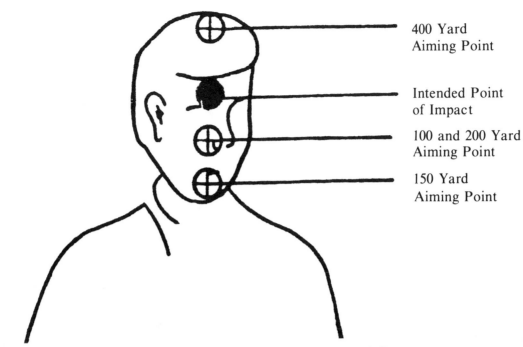

400 Yard
Aiming Point

Intended Point
of Impact

100 and 200 Yard
Aiming Point

150 Yard
Aiming Point

This diagram is based on a weapon that is sighted at a 300-yard distance. The solid circle is the intended point of impact for all shots and is also the aiming point at 300 yards. The circles filled with an X shot where the weapon should be aimed at the given distance. This will allow for the bullet drop or rise and to strike at the intended point of impact.

This type of aiming would not hold true if the weapon is equipped with a range finder. The distance of the shot would be preset on the range finder and the aiming point would always be that of the intended point of impact.

Diagram 4

300 yards, it may be necessary to raise or lower the aiming point depending on the estimated distance of the target. If sighted-in at 300 yards and the target is estimated at approximately 150 yards, the aim will have to be several inches lower or below the intended point of impact. If sighted-in at 300 yards and the target is estimated to be approximately 400 yards, aim will have to be a few inches above the intended point of impact. The distance to allow for the rise and drop of the bullet cannot be precisely determined in any one writing or test by any one caliber of weapon. This is because the caliber and weight of bullets make a difference in the height trajectory of the bullet path (see Diagram Number 4).

All but a very low percentage of shots fired under tactical conditions by the marksman will be at less than 300 yards. Therefore, it is desirable that the potential marksman be prepared to fire at many distances under a variety of circumstances with a minimum amount of mechanical sight changes. To do this, he must have a knowledge of "hold-off." Hold-off is the method previously mentioned where the aiming point is higher or lower than the intended point of impact.

Extensive tests were conducted by M.T.U. to determine the known distance at which the sniper rifle, Remington model 700 equipped with the Redfield scope, variable power (3 to 9), accurange with 18-inch reference wire, should be zeroed to allow the shooter to cover the greatest possible distance to the target without making any mechanical sight changes. This sighting distance was determined to be 500 yards. With a rifle zeroed at this range, the marksman need not hold the cross-hair of the scope off the body of an erect man, since the drop of the bullet between 500 and 600 yards is about 26 inches, while the highest point of trajectory with this sight setting is about 21 inches.

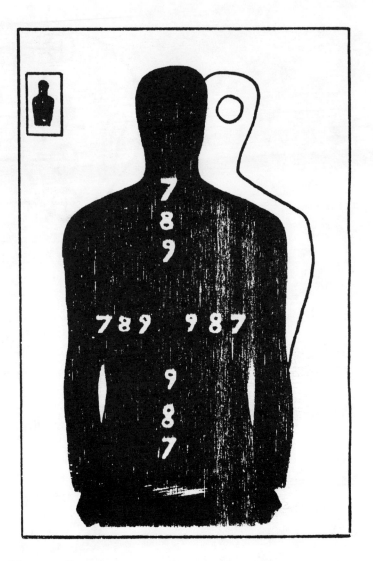

HOSTAGE TAKER PRACTICE TARGET

Standard B-27 target with suspect outline drawn on target background. Intended point of impact circled in suspect outline.

Diagram 5

These tests were conducted for sniper military combat use, and these distances or the ability of the department sniper to hit the main mass of a suspect's body may not be exact enough for a police sniper. The main difference between military sniper conditions and a police tactical situation is that the police must use a much more controlled type of fire. A police sniper may be confronted with a hostage situation in which the main mass of a suspect's body is not visible, and the sniper may have to concentrate on a one-shot kill of the small amount of area that a suspect may expose. It is advisable for the department to pick a sniper weapon and one type of ammunition and practice the one-shot kill method. This can be accomplished using a standard silhouette target and placing a suspect outline to one side of the main target.

With the department weapon sighted in at a certain distance, have all team members practice firing at this type of target starting at the 50-yard line and working their way up to the 300-yard line without changing the sight adjustments. It is imperative that all team members fire a 100 percent into the kill zone. Being involved in a tactical situation under controlled conditions makes selective fire imperative. These situations leave no room for a careless miss that could stray and hit an innocent person.

Practicing with the chemical agent projectile calls for an empty building in an open area away from the public. The CN or CS gas will dissipate in a short while but can be carried by the wind and become a problem if civilians are near the practice area. Show the team what penetrating powers the projectile has and allow the team to experience exposure to the gas. This is also a good time to practice the use of protective equipment (gas mask).

Practicing with burning type canisters of chemical agents should be conducted in an open field free of dry grass or leaves. All team members should practice using the launcher and be familiar with the trajectory of the chemical agent canister.

Show how wind direction will determine where smoke canisters should be placed to accommodate the objective, whether to saturate a crowd with smoke or to use smoke to conceal the team's position or movement.

It might be useful to place an old stuffed chair or mattress in the field and show the effects of a burning canister on combustible items. This would dramatize why it is dangerous to use this type of canister inside a building or where combustibles are present.

Do not waste ammunition on fun firing. All training practice should be done with an objective in mind. This will instill the importance of controlled weapons fire in the minds of the team members. The old adage still stands that there is no room for horseplay at a firing range, whether open field, empty building, or department firing range.

Diagram 6

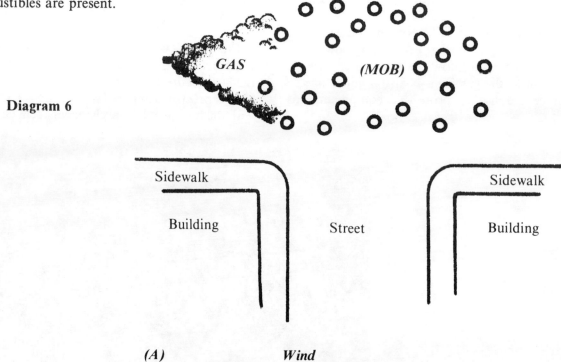

Diagram (A) shows the use of gas and wind to saturate a crowd or mob.

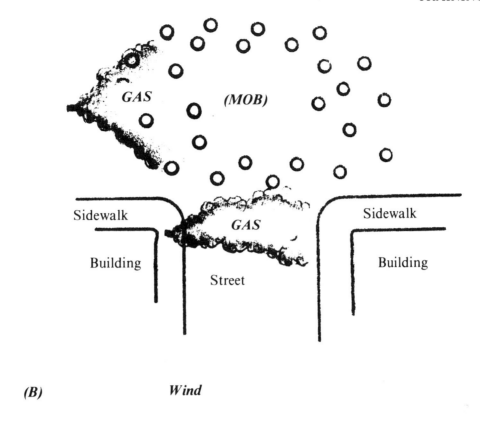

(B)   *Wind*

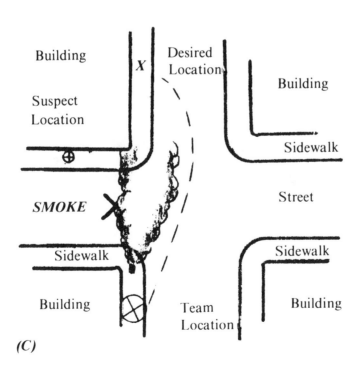

(C)

Diagram (B) shows the use of wind to direct the gas not only into the mob but into the area you do not want the mob to travel.

Diagram (C) shows how to use the wind to direct smoke to cover the area the team may travel without being seen. Be sure to have one team member keep the suspect located.

CLIMBING AND RAPPELLING TECHNIQUES

After team members have undergone some defense training and firearms training, their egos should be nicely under sail. Now is when their sails may get taken in, as their strength and ability are tested. All will remember how in grade school or high school they all climbed the rope in the physical education class. I suggest that they stop to realize that was many years ago, probably before all the good home-cooked meals and countless hours in the patrol car. Unless they have remained in top physical condition or early on taken seriously the benefits of physical exercise, they will probably have to work extra hard in this area before achieving any degree of perfection. One of the main ingredients in the proper use of the ropes is gaining confidence in the ropes. For this reason, practice should begin with the rope and hook climbing.

The rope connected to the hook should be knotted approximately every 12 to 14 inches. The first practice will be throwing the hook. Pick a location that will allow at least a two-story throw (approximately 20 feet).

Hold the rope below the hook at the first knot. Swing the hook with the arm fully extended. Knowing when to release for a good throw will depend on the individual. Practice is the only way to improve each officer's performance.

Climbing can be accomplished in two different methods. One is using the upper body strength, climbing hand over hand, knot to knot with feet against the wall for balance.

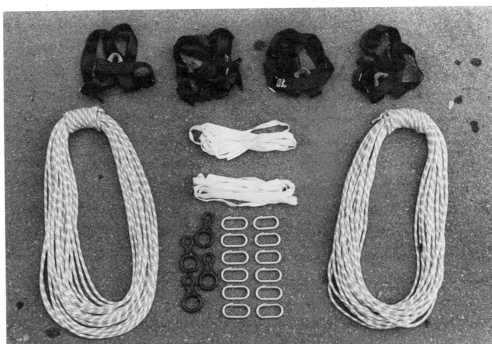

Top row: 4 guide harnesses; Left and right side: 150-foot 11-mm rope; Center top: two 20-foot pieces nylon tubing; Center left: 4 figure-eight descender rings; Center right: 12 carabiners (D-rings).

Another method is to use the hand-over-hand technique with feet gripping the rope and assisting the climb with the leg muscles. Either way will require much endurance and practice. In order to prevent injuries, team members should not allow themselves to become fatigued while climbing. When the rope is thrown and ready to be climbed, two officers should test the position of the hook for proper strength.

Rappelling is another form of rope work that many tactical units find interesting and at times necessary during certain situations. Anytime when the tactical unit is activated to handle a situation located in a multi-story building, rappelling techniques may come into play. Rappelling may be a quick and quiet means of descending to and gaining entry into a building where least expected.

When talking about the equipment to use for rappelling, I must emphasize **proper equipment**. When equipping a team for rappelling, keep in mind that the chance of the entire team having to rappell during one situation will most likely never occur. Gathering equipment for four members of an eight-man team will probably be more than

sufficient. One of the first pieces of equipment to obtain is the rappelling rope. Not just any rope will do the job. There are ropes that are designed solely for this type of activity. Using a rope not designed for this work is a grave risk. The most highly recommended rope for this use is a seven-sixteenths-inch static line caving rope with minimal elasticity. Other equipment will include carabiners (D-rings), figure-eight descender rings, nylon tubing material, and heavy leather gloves. This equipment can be found where rock climbing or mountain climbing equipment is sold. No rappelling equipment should be substituted with hardware store specials.

Pictured in the photograph is the equipment for a four-man rappelling team.

To begin your rappel training, choose a location or building no higher than ten or fifteen feet. The wall being used should be free of windows, doors, or any obstacles that a rappeller may trip over or become tangled in. Your training site must also have an anchor point that will not pull loose under rope pressure or possibly cut the rope. Once you have established the location for the rappel training, place the rope for the rappel.

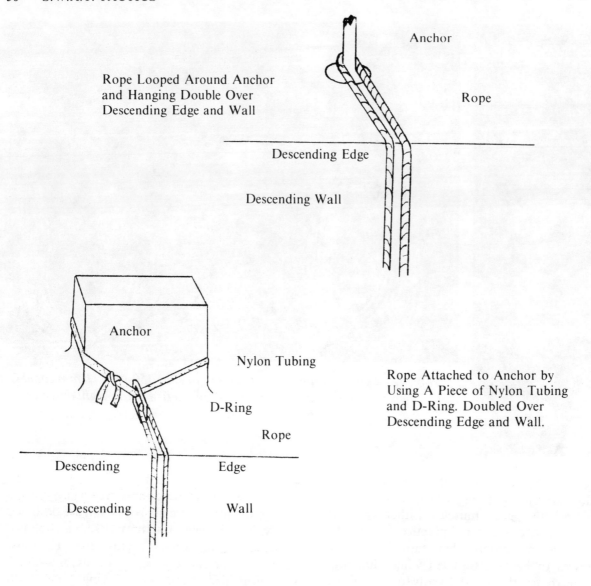

Rope Looped Around Anchor
and Hanging Double Over
Descending Edge and Wall

Anchor

Rope

Descending Edge

Descending Wall

Anchor

Nylon Tubing

D-Ring

Rope

Descending   Edge

Descending   Wall

Rope Attached to Anchor by
Using A Piece of Nylon Tubing
and D-Ring. Doubled Over
Descending Edge and Wall.

Attaching the Rope to Two
Anchor Points Allows the
Rope to Descend in an Area
Other than that Directly
Below a Single Anchor
Point

Diagram 7

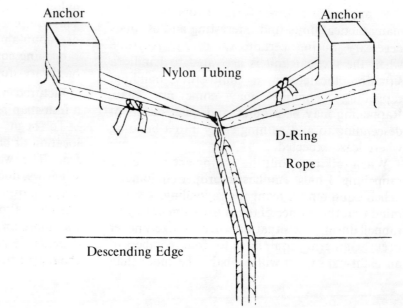

Anchor

Anchor

Nylon Tubing

D-Ring

Rope

Descending Edge

Place the center of the rappelling rope around the anchor to allow the rope to hang double over the wall. If this is not possible, you may have to use a piece of the nylon tubing secured to one or more anchor points. Attach the rope to the tubing with the use of a D-ring.

Once the rope is in place, get into the harness and be sure all harness straps and buckles are tight. For an extra measure of safety, run the harness strap ends back through the buckles a second time to assure against slipping. To connect the harness to the rappelling rope, you will use two D-rings and a figure-eight descender ring.

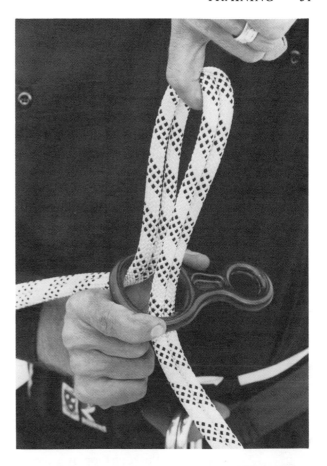

Place two D-rings in the harness loop with the D-ring gates side by side and opening in the same direction.

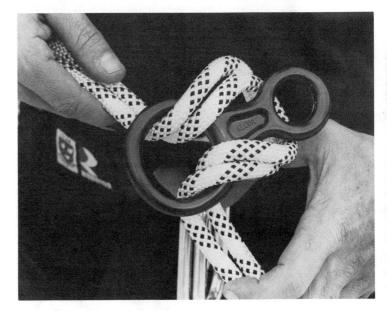

Connect the figure-eight descender ring to the rappelling rope by pushing the rappelling rope through the larger figure-eight ring hole. Now place the loop formed in the rope over the smaller end of the figure-eight ring and pull the rope until it is snug against the neck of the figure-eight ring.

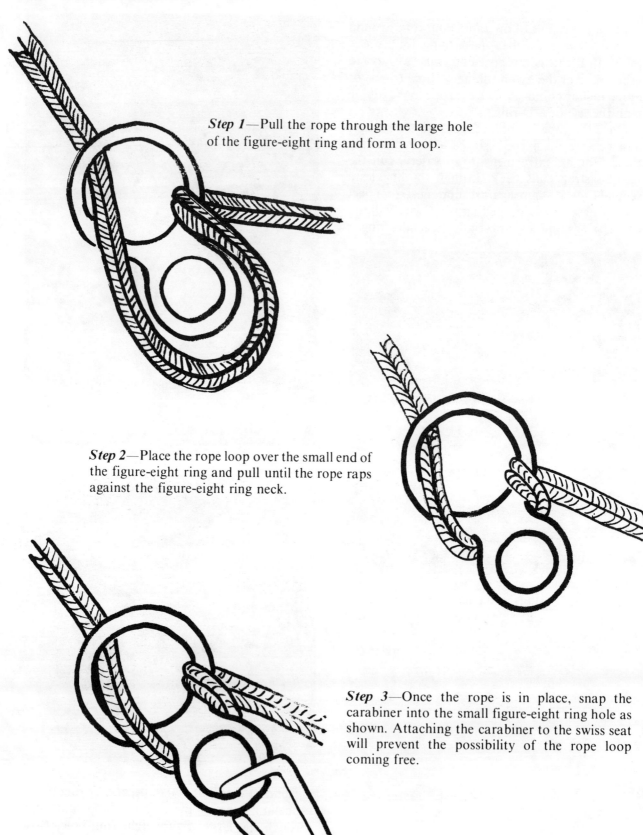

Step 1—Pull the rope through the large hole of the figure-eight ring and form a loop.

Step 2—Place the rope loop over the small end of the figure-eight ring and pull until the rope raps against the figure-eight ring neck.

Step 3—Once the rope is in place, snap the carabiner into the small figure-eight ring hole as shown. Attaching the carabiner to the swiss seat will prevent the possibility of the rope loop coming free.

Diagram 8

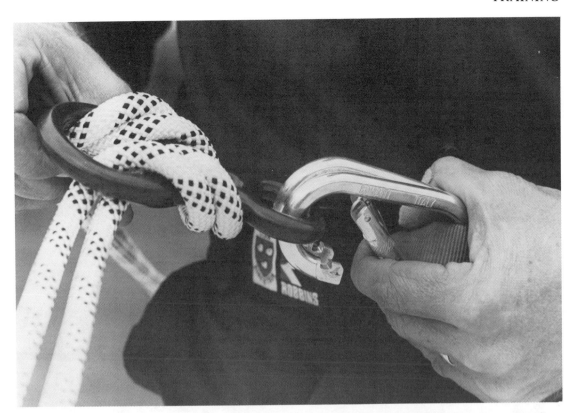

Snap the small hole of the figure-eight descender ring into the two D-rings that are on the harness. Once snapped in, turn one D-ring over so that the D-ring gates are on opposite sides.

Locking D-rings are available but are not recommended for tactical use due to the possibility of this type of ring becoming jammed. Jamming prevents opening and stops you from being able to disconnect. Put on the leather gloves to protect your hands from rope burns.

Now lean out over the descending edge, allowing the rope to hold your weight. Do not let go of your grip with the brake hand. To descend, you allow the rope to slide through the braking hand.

Stand with your back to the descending edge. Take hold of the rope trailing behind you, and with your strong hand pull the rope to your rear. This hand position is referred to as the braking hand. Now take hold of the rope that extends between you and the anchor with your weak hand, which is referred to as the balance hand. Be sure that the rope between you and the anchor is pulled tight. At this point you are ready to begin. This is the spot with which most beginners have the greatest trouble. Placc your feet approximately one shoulder-width apart, and hold tight with the braking hand.

Once you lean far enough for your body to form an L-shape, bending at the waist and with your legs fairly straight, step over the descending edge. Allow your weight and leverage with the rope to hold you against the wall until you have descended far enough to allow the rappelling rope to rest atop the descending edge.

At this point it is just a matter of a steady walk down the wall, controlling your descending speed with your braking hand. During a descent, you may find it necessary to stop and maintain a certain position for a length of time. One method you may use calls for nothing more than an extra D-ring and your ability to handle the rope.

Once you have stopped your descent with your braking hand, reach around with your balance hand and pull the rope around your waist. Wrap

the rope around your upper leg two times, and then snap the rope into the extra D-ring attached to the harness. To continue descending, be sure

your braking hand is in its original position, unsnap the rope from the extra D-ring, and unwrap the rope from your leg.

There are many techniques that can be used with rappelling and rope equipment other than the straight descent that is shown in this chapter. I would suggest that professional rappel guidance and training be sought for team members.

4
Training for Tactical Situations

This chapter considers the tactical situations S.W.A.T. teams normally face and is a general introduction to training for them. No book could cover every potential situation, or even every detail of a few possible encounters. What this chapter is meant to provide is a guide for training and models for role playing.

Part of training should include role-playing tactical situations, that is, mock trial runs. I cannot stress enough the importance of this kind of practice. It is when you begin to role play tactical situations that you learn how easy it is to make fatal mistakes. In one of my very first sessions of training, I was "shot" in the face while searching for our "suspect." I made a mistake that I will not make again. Others on our team have learned the same.

For role playing, the team leader and members can use their imagination in setting up situations. There is, of course, an element of play in this, so it is one of the more enjoyable exercises in team training. The play aspect also allows for the use of friends or other department members to act as suspects and hostages. It is important, however, to remember a couple of things about this type of role-playing training.

One is that, although it is playing, the team members are learning. They need to keep in mind that practicing the techniques of tactical control and survival must be done energetically and with concentration. How they practice the techniques in training by role playing will largely determine how they will do them in real-life situations. Do not let the play aspect lead to sloppy practice.

On the other hand, do not lose the play aspect. This is the second important thing to remember. I said that team members should practice the role playing "energetically and with concentration." I did not say they should take it "seriously." Those familiar with the "playing" of sports and social scientists familiar with role-playing experiments know how easy it is for people to forget they are role playing and to start taking the situation seriously—as if it were for real—and to start acting as if they were in a real-life situation. Certainly it is understood that live ammunition is **never** used in these mock tactical situations. Nevertheless, an overly eager and anxious kick to the groin of a friend, who volunteered to be a "suspect," is unwelcome, unnecessary, and only possible if someone's distinction between reality and playing gets blurred. Every team member should be briefed about the possibility of this blurring; consciousness of the problem is the best preventive measure.

Role-playing tactical situations requires a place, and almost any place will do. Large farms, fields, and forests are good for this. We have used a large farm with a number of farm buildings to some advantage. Other places are also possibilities, such as the top floor of a hotel or the police department's basement. For example, we sent one man with a "hostage" to the top floor of a local hotel (with the owner's permission, of course). Our "suspect" was armed with a .22-caliber blank starter pistol, which is particularly useful for this kind of thing since nothing comes out of the barrel; otherwise, I could have been burned when he "shot" me in the face. Another time, we chased a "suspect" with a rubber knife into the basement of the police station.

What is very important for such role playing is that there not be people around who do not know what is going on and may think there is really some police action taking place. This is a problem that must be worked out in all particulars before the role playing is begun and especially in highly populated areas.

SITUATIONS

Probably the most common situation encountered is the barricaded suspect (s). The common image of this is a person who has piled furniture in front of the doors and windows, is heavily armed, and is awaiting the arrival of the police for a final showdown. This type of barricaded situation is rare, and when it does occur, much planning has usually been done on both sides, police and suspect(s) alike, and will be handled by the larger, more well-equipped tactical units.

The small department tactical units are more likely to be confronted with a suspect who, in the act of bungling a crime, has been discovered by local police and has, therefore, had to take refuge at some nearby location. Sometimes this person will use people in the same area as hostages, in hopes of negotiating his escape. Unless this person is pursued to his residence, he will usually be armed with only enough firepower to commit the originally planned crime and will not have enough equipment to give much resistance.

Perhaps an easier definition of a barricaded suspect is one who uses cover or concealment to assist in avoiding capture by the police. One may also find this type of situation developing in homes where there is a family crisis, and one member of the family is suffering from severe emotional instability. (See Appendix A for a few remarks regarding general psychological types encountered in tactical situations.)

Another situation that may be encountered by small departments is the sniper. The sniper can best be described as a more or less expert marksman who is usually concealed and uses a long-range weapon against his "enemy" at the greatest distance possible. Snipers' weapons have included everything from the bow and arrow to a high-powered rifle with a telescopic sight. Sniping is also used during riots and civil disorders as a tactical maneuver against police and others authorized to bring the disorder under control.

Sniping has, at least in the past, been a favorite tool of the assassin. It is effective in that it allows the sniper to remain at a distance from his victim and thus, because of the confusion, allows time for the sniper's escape. Sniping has also been an act of the emotionally disturbed; such may fire at will against anyone that can be seen.

One problem that a tactical team may be faced with is that the sniper sometimes will not stay in one place long enough for the team to be deployed to the location. This will be dealt with in the "Situation Control" section that follows.

The third situation a team may encounter is an ambush attack. An ambush attack may be described as a close-to-intermediate range attack against the person or area being protected by team members, or a close-range attack on the team itself. This is not a usual occurrence when dealing with common criminals or the emotionally disturbed. One is more likely to run into an ambush attack when attempting to regain order during a civil disturbance (riot) or when dealing with terrorism. During a riot, the ambush attack is usually designed to maintain a state of confusion among riot control officers and prevent order from being restored. This has been a popular means for one or another organization to gain recognition during a riot situation.

These are just a few situations that would probably be handled by the tactical team. The tactical team could also be deployed in other circumstances, especially where potential tactical situations could develop, such as the serving of some warrants, stakeouts, drug raids, et cetera. The use of the tactical team in these situations would not only be beneficial to the department, but would also give the team more opportunities to work together as a unit to allow for a better understanding of each other's individual habits and personalities.

SITUATION CONTROL

Situation control does not begin upon the arrival of the armed tactical unit. Once an assignment has taken the shape of a tactical situation, a certain amount of time will be needed to deploy a team. During this time of preparation, certain actions must be taken by the officer(s) on the scene. This is an area that needs to be brought to the attention of the entire department by the tactical team.

Barricaded Suspect

The early responsibility concerning the situation of a barricaded suspect will fall on the shoulders of the first officer on the scene. Such a situation usually develops from a response to a radio assignment by a regular patrol officer or detective. Assignments with the greatest potential to become a barricaded situation are silent alarms, serving of warrants, and family disputes. The first officer on the scene when such a situation develops must set the command response in motion by notifying his immediate commander.

Once this is done, the first officer must take the necessary steps needed to contain the situation in the smallest area possible. This must be accomplished without necessitating a confrontation with the suspect. If there is another escape route that the suspect may use, another road officer must take up a position to eliminate the possibility. This area now contained by the two road officers is referred to as an inner perimeter.

The inner perimeter must be maintained by these officers until relieved by tactical team members. Strict weapons control must be maintained, and action should be taken only in the event that the situation would escalate proving a threat to human life, and only when immediate action is required to save human life.

Once the commanding officer has responded and has determined that a tactical situation does exist, he should notify the department or area negotiating team and the tactical unit. This being done, the commanding officer should take steps to further contain the situation by forming an outer perimeter.

The outer perimeter can be described as a buffer zone; it is the area directly surrounding the inner perimeter. The outer perimeter must be large enough to prevent onlookers and bystanders from wandering into a dangerous situation and to give the tactical team room to maneuver without entering the inner perimeter. All vehicle and pedestrian traffic must be kept out of the outer and inner perimeters. This would include the press, medical, or other personnel who may think they have reason for being in the area. The only persons that should be let through the outer perimeter guard would be those cleared by the negotiator or the tactical team commander.

This may seem like a great many duties to be handled by regular duty officers, but in reality only a few minutes will have passed, and the situation will already be somewhat under control.

Sniper

The sniper is a tactical problem that does not always allow time for the activation or arrival of a tactical team. At times snipers will even use hit-and-run tactics, which makes pinpointing the origin of fire extremely difficult. Another hardship in locating a sniper is caused by the sound of his weapon echoing off surrounding structures, or by the sound being covered up or drowned out by traffic noise or other noises around the officer under fire. An officer under sniper attack should immediately drive out of the line of fire. If this is not possible due to traffic or logistic reasons, the officer should abandon his vehicle and run to a place of safety. Officers should never consider their auto as protective cover from sniper fire. There are very few, if any, automobiles on the road today that offer any ballistic protection from incoming rifle rounds, and climbing under the car will leave one vulnerable to ricochet off the pavement.

The officer under attack should then notify his commander of the situation and, without exposing himself to more gunfire, try to determine the origin of the sniper fire. If this is not possible, he should remain in a place of safety and alert any officers in the area to the situation, so they can avoid becoming victims of the sniper. The commander on duty must immediately notify the tactical team and have road officers start redirecting vehicle and pedestrian traffic from the area.

If the location of the sniper has been determined, road officers should attempt only to block his avenues of escape. Road officers should not confront the sniper, since the sniper's firepower is likely greater than that of the officers. Any

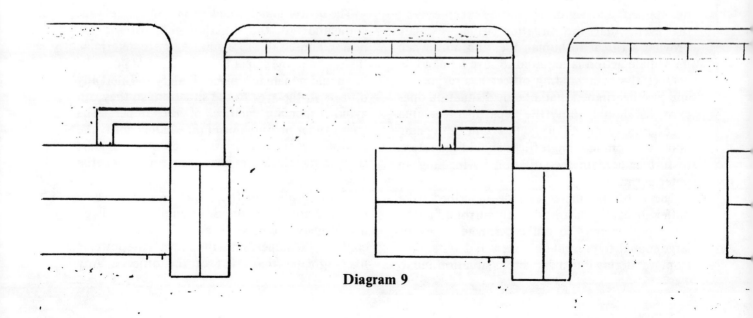

(2)

(B)

SUSPECT
LOCATION

(A)

(1)

Figures 1 and 2 show the location of the first and
second officers on the scene. The uneven line
shows the area contained within the inner
perimeter.

Diagram 9

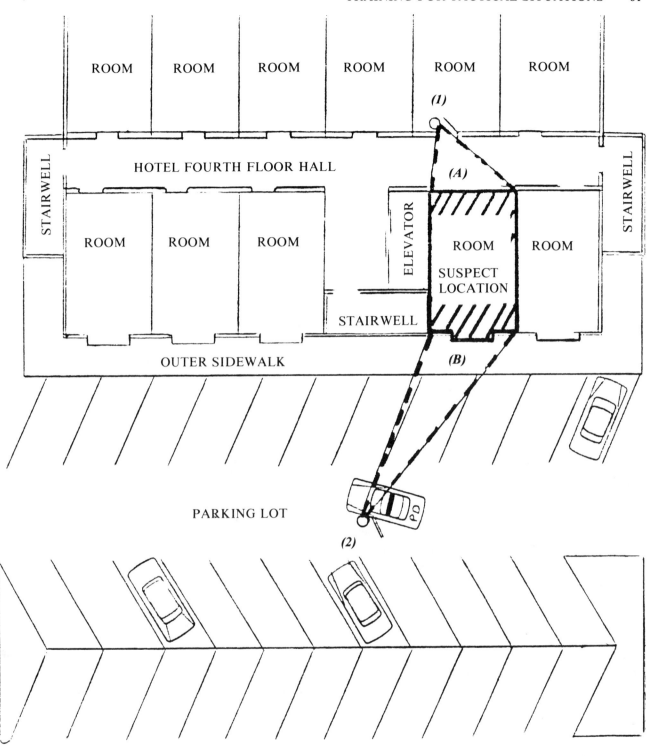

Areas marked A and B indicate the area within the inner perimeter.

Figure 1 indicates first officers' location to form the first part of the inner perimeter.

Figure 2 is the location secured by the second officer due to the outer hotel room window.

Diagram 10

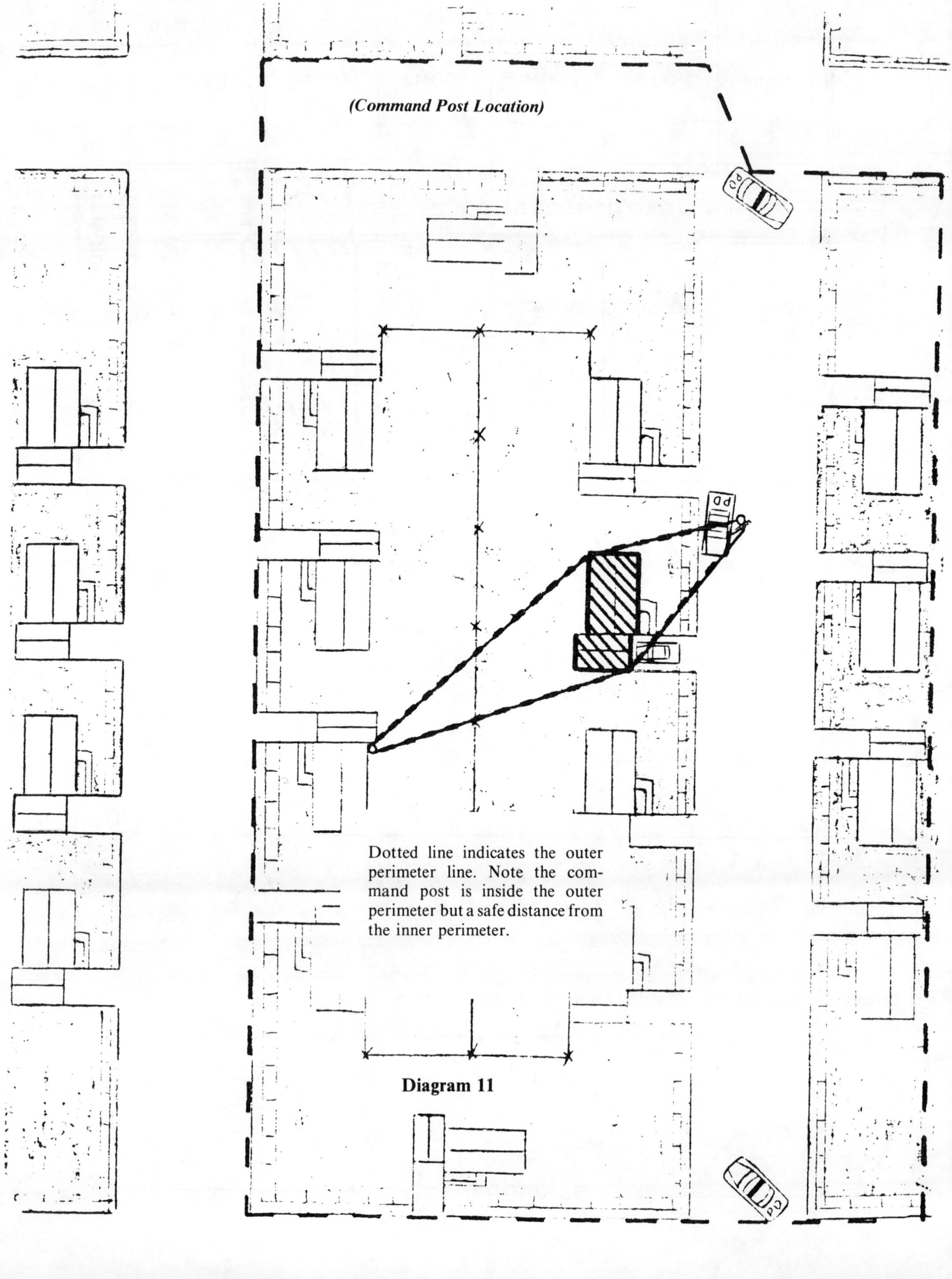

(Command Post Location)

Dotted line indicates the outer
perimeter line. Note the command post is inside the outer
perimeter but a safe distance from
the inner perimeter.

Diagram 11

confrontation or return fire should be left to the tactical team. Road officers trying to return sniper fire with their handguns or shotguns would only produce a more dangerous situation than the one already existing. Blocking the avenues of escape and preventing others from entering the area of the sniper will give the best control of the situation until the arrival of the tactical team.

Ambush Attack

As a rule, there is no time to summon assistance from a tactical team when a road officer is ambushed. This is a situation that will have to be dealt with accordingly. An ambush can best be described as a close to intermediate surprise attack, preplanned, for the purpose of causing confusion in the area of an already developed situation. Sometimes it is done to bring notoriety to a particular group, especially to show that they have control over the lives of those being attacked.

A tactical team must remain alert to being drawn into an ambush when handling other assignments. A suspect may purposely cause a tactical situation by placing himself in a location that would cause the tactical team to approach an area where an ambush is lying in wait. This is especially true when the tactical team is working a situation where the suspect belongs to a group such as an outlaw motorcycle gang, a known terrorist organization, or any group large enough to launch such an attack.

Another situation in which the tactical unit is vulnerable to an ambush attack is when assisting in a crowd or riot control situation. This is when the ambush attack may not be for the purpose of taking the lives of officers but for the purpose of creating more confusion and adding hostility toward the officers, especially by causing an overreaction by the police. Last but not least is when the tactical team is performing VIP protection or guarding some type of installation, such as a government building or public facility during a civil disorder. This again may not be for the purpose of taking the officers' lives, but for taking control of whom or what the officers are protecting.

Similar to a sniper attack, there is no time for discussing a plan of action or setting up negotiations. Immediate action must be taken as soon as the attack is launched. More will be said about this in the next section.

TACTICAL RESPONSE AND SURVIVAL TECHNIQUES

Barricaded Suspect

When responding to a barricaded suspect situation, no team member should take any action until the entire responding unit has arrived and been briefed. The only time this would not hold true is if immediate action must be taken to save human life.

Once the tactical unit has assembled at the designated command post and has been briefed on the necessary details, team members should move in to re-establish the inner perimeter, which had previously been formed by the assignment responding road officers. Remember that some time has elapsed since the arrival of the first officer, and the suspect may be better prepared for the unit's arrival. While moving into or around the inner perimeter, make use of any and all cover and concealment. Concealment is an area or object that conceals or hides the officer's location but offers little or no ballistic protection. Cover is an area or object that not only offers concealment but also complete ballistic protection.

When advancing to a location, concealment should be considered only as a temporary stop before moving on to proper cover. When you are using concealment and you are fired upon, the only recourse for survival is to return the fire. When in a proper place offering good cover, fire need not be returned. Whenever possible, it is good to use proper cover for protection and let the suspect waste and possibly run out of ammunition.

Using proper cover improperly renders the cover or location useless. One should use to good advantage any darkened areas, shadows, or irregular backgrounds.

This officer was the first officer on the scene and sought proper ballistic cover. The object he is using for cover will offer all the protection needed against hostile fire. The two points of concern with this location, however, are that the officer has no avenue of escape if needed, and he is very vulnerable when he tries to observe the suspect's location.

A more distant location of cover may prove more desirable by offering a vantage point for observation without detection. A more distant location may also offer an avenue of escape.

When moving over obstacles, do so quickly with as little exposure as possible. Thick rows of shrubs and fences provide little or no concealment or cover. Jumping these obstacles in an upright position or taking time to climb them causes unnecessary exposure.

Providing the obstacle is low enough, one may find the diving-roll technique very handy. This keeps exposure time to a minumum and will not block the view of the cover man.

Moving around corners must be done with great care. If one has a mirror, it should be used.

Without a mirror, look quickly from a low position. Pull back and then look quickly again from another higher position.

Once it is determined that the area is clear for advancement, do so under the cover of another team member. One person should move in a low position with the cover above him. It is important that the first man never line himself up directly in front of the cover man. Whatever space is available should be used to keep separate and to keep a clear view for firing.

Wrong

Right

Once the inner perimeter is established by the tactical unit, the team marksman should establish a vantage point for observation. Usually the marksman will have best results from high ground. In residential areas, for example, a rooftop overlooking the suspect's location is a good vantage point. When a rooftop is used, the marksman must take care not to be silhouetted at the peak of the building.

A position accompanied by irregular lines, such as a chimney, should be selected. Using objects behind the roof to aid in concealment is also advisable. If none of these concealing aids are available, the idea of the rooftop should be abandoned.

If the marksman chooses a position inside, using a window for a vantage point, the weapon should not be allowed to protrude from the window. Also, one should be aware of light shining in the window or light coming from the back, either of which could give the marksman's position away. It might be necessary to set up deep inside the room against an inner wall or against room furniture.

Once the inner perimeter is secured and the team marksman is set for observation, the road officers are relieved from the inner perimeter positions, and the other team members should try to remove any injured, wounded, or other innocent persons caught inside the inner area. When the area is cleared and contained, a course of action must be chosen. There are various considerations when planning what action to take.

According to G. Wayne Fuselier:

Whenever a barricaded suspect or hostage situation exists, the following responses are available to law enforcement personnel:

(1) Contain and attempt to negotiate;
(2) Contain and demand surrender;
(3) Use of chemical agents to force surrender;
(4) Use of snipers or sharpshooters to neutralize the subject;
(5) Use of a special weapons and tactical assault (S.W.A.T.).[1]

When these alternatives are considered, it is usually better to progress from one of the earlier responses to the later responses. But remember that it is almost impossible to return to negotiating, especially after an assault has taken place.

Once the situation is contained and negotiations have begun, the tactical unit will maintain its position and take no action unless advised to do so by the command post. The command post will determine if the negotiations are deteriorating or if the situation is becoming uncontrollably violent.

Negotiations have been known to go on for many hours. This could lead to fatigue on the part of tactical officers maintaining certain positions. If negotiations do drag on, arrangements should be made to relieve members at regular intervals. During the negotiating period, more detailed plans can be designed by the tactical team.

A situation including hostages is considerably more complex. The hostages themselves are likely to play an important part in the negotiating process. Of course, hostages react differently when first faced with the reality of being taken hostage, but in time, unless grossly mistreated by the hostage-taker(s), hostages tend to develop a common set of feelings identified as the Stockholm Syndrome. The syndrome consists of one or more of the following:

(1) The hostages begin to have a positive feeling toward the hostage-taker or toward the reasoning used by the hostage-taker.
(2) The hostages begin to develop ill feelings toward the authorities.
(3) The hostage-taker(s) begin to have positive feelings toward the hostages and the situation in which they have been placed.

All hostages will not be affected to the same degree, but it should be assumed that some portion of the syndrome will develop as time passes.

From the standpoint of the negotiator, the Stockholm Syndrome works in his favor. If categories (1) and (2) occur, there is less chance that a hostage will take action that will cause the hostage-taker to harm or kill the hostages. If the third category occurs, there is little chance that the hostage-taker will want to harm the hostages.

---

[1] G. Wayne Fuselier, Ph.D., "A Practical Overview of Hostage Negotiations," *FBI Law Enforcement Bulletin*, June 1981, Part 1.

The problem with the Stockholm Syndrome comes when the negotiations break down and the tactical unit has to take action. Any information coming from the hostages may be false information. This false information may be deliberate, or it may be given unconsciously. When the tactical team sets a plan of action into motion, these plans should not rely on any assistance from the hostages. The syndrome may cause the hostages to counter any commands given by rescuing officers. There have been incidents documented in which hostages who had been released and taken to a place of safety made their way back and resumed their position as hostages.

In the event that the hostages have been mistreated, any information gained from them could be greatly exaggerated, such as weapons being used or stated intentions of the hostage-taker. It is important that such information not be taken as fact. Exaggerated information could cause an overreaction on the part of team members, because they may then expect much more of a threat than actually exists.

One other point to keep in mind is that the negotiator himself is not totally immune to the Stockholm Syndrome. For this reason it is important that the negotiator not be a part of the tactical assault unit. Also, any communications between the negotiator and the tactical unit should be through the command post. Exploited wisely, the Stockholm Syndrome can actually help achieve the ultimate objective, which is the safe release of the hostages.

I have been discussing considerations to take into account while the team plans its action. There are also some guidelines to follow when deciding what plan of action to take if negotiations fail. The first is to demand the release of the hostages and the surrender of the suspect. Here it might be wise to deploy part of the team to show the suspect that his escape is impossible and that the team has the ability to neutralize him by force if necessary.

Nevertheless, the suspect's emotional stability must be kept in mind, that is, if it is at all known. A show of force without immediate action could cause more harm than good. If the suspect is suffering from a particularly severe character disorder, action may have to be taken as soon as the negotiations break down.

If the situation exists in which hostages are present or other persons in the area could fall victim to an assault by the team, the team marksman should be ready to fire on the suspect. In this course of action, there should be only one shot fired—that of the marksman. In the event that the marksman does not have a clean shot or a clear field of fire, the cover, armed with a semiautomatic rifle, may have to assume the task of marksman. In either event, the assault team should be ready to move the instant the team's first shot is fired.

If there are no hostages or if the hostages have been kept isolated from the suspect, the use of chemical agents can be deployed to either force the suspect from his barricaded position or even to surrender. Try never to subject hostages to the chemical agents. There is always the possibility of suffocation, and the hostages may be injured or kept in a way that would prevent them from moving out of the area where the chemical agent has been applied.

In conjunction with the decision to use chemical agents is the selection of the exit desired for the suspect. Have that exit well covered by tactical team members, and use the chemical agent to drive the suspect to the desired exit. This is accomplished by saturating the area most distant from the desired exit with gas and by working the saturation toward the exit.

If dealing with a two- or three-story building, begin by saturating the upper floors with gas, driving the suspect to the ground floor or keeping him from moving to the upper floors in an attempt to escape the assault.

Be ready for a possible violent confrontation when the suspect exits the building. In the event that the suspect refuses to exit after the use of gas, the tactical team will have to be equipped with protective equipment and move in to take control of the suspect and move the hostages to a place of safety and fresh air. The suspect's ability to defend his position should be greatly reduced by the effects of the gas, and overtaking him should not be too difficult.

The last alternative is for the tactical unit to launch an assault on the suspect's location. If there are no hostages present, a diversion can be set up by the negotiator or by the command post while team members quietly move in on the suspect's location. Once in, the shock of the team's presence might be enough in itself to cause the suspect to surrender.

When launching an assault, make use of all cover and concealment possible, as previously described. One thing to remember is that very few

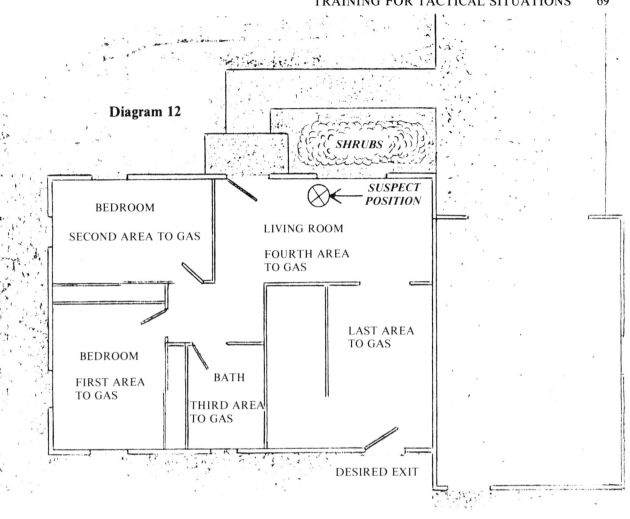

Diagram 12

SHRUBS

⊗ ← **SUSPECT POSITION**

BEDROOM

SECOND AREA TO GAS

LIVING ROOM

FOURTH AREA TO GAS

LAST AREA TO GAS

BEDROOM

FIRST AREA TO GAS

BATH

THIRD AREA TO GAS

DESIRED EXIT

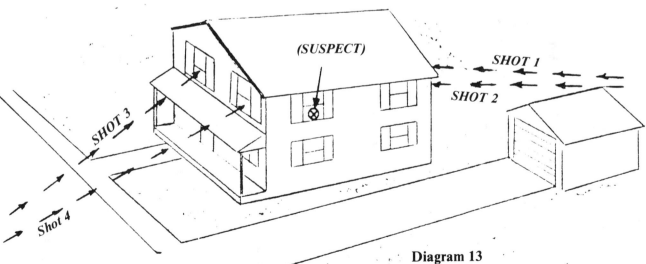

(SUSPECT)

SHOT 1

SHOT 2

SHOT 3

Shot 4

Diagram 13

In the above situation where a suspect is located on an upper floor, gas would be delivered simultaneously in the order shown. This technique would not only force the suspect from his present location but would prevent his taking refuge in another upper floor room. The only area not directly saturated with gas would be the hall and stairway. Because of the eventual expansion of gas to this area, the only avenue of escape would be to a lower floor. At this point you would follow the set plan to force the suspect to the desired exit.

interior structures, such as an interior wall, provide ballistic protection. If the suspect is aware of an officer's location, he may be able to fire through the wall. Consequently, once the assault is begun, all team members must be ready to act fast and move in quickly to neutralize the suspect's ability to resist. This is especially true when hostages are present. Not only must the team be concerned with the suspect taking refuge behind the hostages, but also with hostages, under the effects of the Stockholm Syndrome, warning the suspect of the team's presence.

When an assault is in progress, the team members must beware of obstacles or booby traps set by the suspect. Such traps can be anything from something as simple as a staircase rigged to collapse to a more sophisticated explosive device attached to trip wires or to a light switch. One of the latest booby traps to be encountered was a two-liter soda bottle tilted on its side and filled one-third with concentrated sulfuric acid mixed with two cups of gasoline. Hanging inside the bottle, from the screw-on top, was a dry, empty tea bag filled with potassium chlorate. As soon as the bottle is tipped over, it becomes an instant "super molotov cocktail," erupting into a large and instantaneous fireball.[2]

If assaulting a position in a multi-story building, try to enter from an upper floor. For such an assault, the hook and rope could be of great help. Knowing the suspect's location inside the building makes entry much safer. Try to cover the entry noise with a greater noise away from the entry but near the suspect. Using a police siren or the public address system will give good cover noise.

Rappelling might be the easiest and quickest means to reach some locations on the building. Handling or firing a weapon from the rope while rappelling is very difficult, to say the least. The officers should be positioned so that they do not have to defend themselves while on the rope. Once inside the structure, the use of hand signals might be the safest and most quiet means of communicating among the officers. (See Appendix B for hand signal techniques.)

---

[2]"Survival School," *Police Product News*, May 1982.

When moving into a hallway, do not commit more than two officers at a time. The cover should take up a position while the unit defense moves ahead. Even if the suspect's location is known, it is advisable to search every room for confederates of the suspect. Once a room is searched, use a small piece of tape and mark the door. If it is necessary to return through that particular area, the tape can be "read" as to whether the doorway has been used after the search. If a door must be secured, blocked open, or blocked closed, a wood wedge or nylon line can be used to accomplish this.

Another area that leaves officers particularly vulnerable is a stairwell. Again, only commit two officers at a time; one to advance and one to give cover. Be careful that whoever leads the advance not lead with a weapon sticking out in front. A weapon that sticks out in front of an officer can be taken by the suspect. If the quarters are too tight to properly move around with the rifle or shotgun, sling the gun over one shoulder and use the handgun.

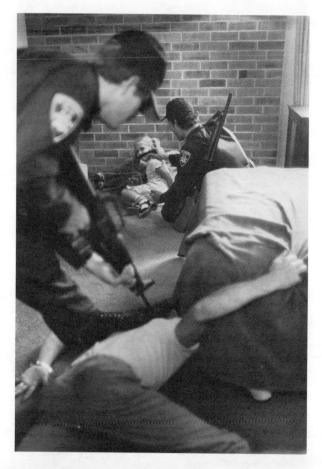

Once the assault has succeeded and the suspect has been neutralized, remove him from the area as quickly as possible. Do not overlook the fact that the hostages could pose a threat. Handle the hostages with care but remain alert. The situation is not over until all involved have been cleared from the area, a final search has been conducted, and the investigative team has started its investigation.

Sniper

A tactical team's response to a sniper situation will differ somewhat from its response to a barricaded suspect. The first responsibility is to prevent the sniper from continuing to fire. This can be accomplished by having the team marksman set up a distracting line of fire that will cause the sniper to take cover. A cover man should be used as an observer. Once the team marksman fires his first shot, there is a good chance that the sniper will know his position and try to return fire. With two officers capable of returning fire, one can return fire while the other observes the sniper's action. This system is used to prevent the sniper from having enough time to set up a clean shot.

If hostages have been taken or other persons are near the sniper's location, distracting fire can be aimed near the sniper, at the window sill, door jam, or ceiling, close enough to cause the sniper to think that he is under fire, yet far enough away to assure the safety of innocent persons. The remainder of the team then launches an immediate assault on the sniper's location. It follows that the same procedures, as well as cautions, are used with a barricaded suspect.

If possible, the marksman's and observer's positions should be at a higher elevation than that of the sniper. This will assist the other team members, since the sniper's attention will be on the movement of the marksman. A must for the marksman is a set location or stationary position with complete ballistic protection and an avenue of escape.

Ambush

When ambushed, there is no time to deploy a marksman, or even to set up an inner perimeter. The team's actions must be spontaneous. As soon as the team is aware of the ambush, those in the direct line of fire should launch their own attack on the attacker's position. The other team members should seek immediate cover and give cover fire to allow the attacking team members to seek cover.

One of the main problems with attacking an ambusher's position is keeping persons in the area safe, not only from the ambusher's fire but also from that of the officers' counterattack. As far as is possible (if the team is not pinned down by the ambush), after the initial response and all the team has found cover, the situation can be treated as one of hostile fire from a barricaded suspect or a sniper, whichever the case may be.

Riot Control

Tactical teams are also used for riot and crowd control, but a team of the size treated in this text may be too small for situations in which the crowd or riot is especially large. It makes sense, then, for the tactical team to be deployed as a protective force for regular duty officers assigned to form the crowd or riot control line. The proper place for a tactical unit during such a situation would be behind the riot control line and, if possible, above, looking down over the situation.

The unit defense would be in a position directly behind the control line for the purpose of delivering tear gas or another chemical agent if required. The cover would be behind the unit defense to give cover fire if an ambush were to occur or to assist in the arrest of persons who may break the control line. The rear guard would be at the rear of the entire scene to protect the control line from a rear attack and to warn of any possible problem areas that could be developing behind the line. If possible, the team marksman should take up a position above the situation to protect the control line and team members from the possibility of a sniper attack. If a position cannot be attained above the situation, the marksman should find a position that is not directly related to the other team members so as not to be readily detected. A sniper would try first to eliminate the person who poses the greatest threat to him.

This type of deployment would allow the crowd control officers to keep their minds on their objective and the team members to concentrate on the situations they have been trained for.

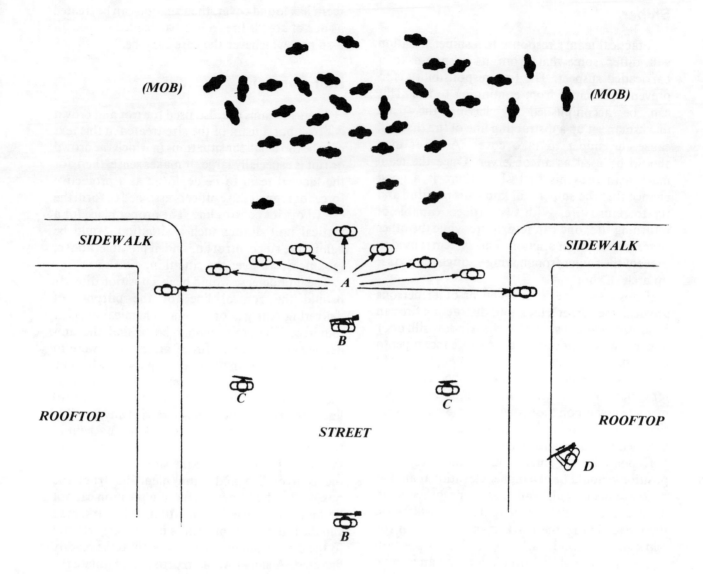

A—Riot Control Squad Armed with Riot Batons

B—Unit Defensemen Armed with Chemical Agent

C—Covermen Armed with Semiautomatic Rifles

D—Marksman Armed with Scoped High-Power Rifle

Diagram 14

5

Conclusion

The material covered here may seem like a great deal of training to learn and to practice. In time, it will be found that many of these techniques are just good common sense and may have been overlooked for one reason or another.

There are, no doubt, many techniques that could be added to this text by training officers; do not hesitate to add them. If it is felt that some of the techniques in this book are impractical or unnecessary, do not disregard them completely. In time, it will be seen that they have their place in certain situations.

Remember that a tactical unit is not developed for urban guerrilla warfare. A civil police tactical unit is for the purpose of handling situations that are not controllable by regular duty officers. The S.W.A.T. team is there for the primary purpose of preventing the needless deaths of not only hostages, innocent persons, and police personnel, but suspects as well.

A tactical team's training never ends. When possible, it is good to work with other departments and other tactical units. Trade ideas and train together. Seek specialized training offered by organizations such as the FBI, police training institutions, and possibly area colleges. Do not feel frustrated if after training for months, or even years, the team is not activated. It is better to have a team and not need it, than to need it and not have it.

Appendix A
Whom to Expect

In handling tactical situations it is beneficial if the team members have some insight into the kinds of personalities they are most likely to encounter.

The most typical person to be encountered is the "common" criminal. This person possesses a normal ability to think and to reason. He becomes involved in a tactical situation when, during the commission of a crime, his plans become fouled for one reason or another, such as the early arrival of the police. His reactions may not appear normal, but they are normal actions to him because of his escalating fear of being taken into custody or, worse, being injured or killed by the police. This type of person usually can be dealt with by a trained negotiator, and the use of a tactical team is primarily for a show of force, which is normally enough to cause his eventual surrender. Hostages taken are seldom harmed due to the suspect's ability to be rational. He realizes that they are the reason an assault has not been launched against him. He realizes that harming the hostages would only compound his problems.

If an assault is necessary, his resistance is usually light, since he possesses only the weapons needed to commit the originally intended crime. But beware—not all persons who bungle a crime are simply common criminals.

Another personality type that the tactical team might encounter falls into the category of the emotionally disturbed. For the sake of simplicity these emotional disorders have been broken down into three categories: the psychotic, the neurotic, and the character disorders.[3]

When one who is suffering from delusions and/or hallucinations takes a hostage, that person, to some degree, sets the rules. He is reacting from what to him is overwhelming stress. He is compelled to take action to relieve that stress. This may include the taking of hostages, even members of his own family. He cannot be appealed to on a rational basis because he does not view the world in a rational way. He may have a sense of mission much like Sam Byck who planned to crash a commercial aircraft into the White House. In January 1974, Byck attempted to carry out his scheme and commandeered an airliner, killed the pilot, wounded the co-pilot, and eventually, when his plan failed, committed suicide. He called his plan "Operation Pandora Box."

A second emotional aberration is a form of severe depression, where the only logical answer

---

[3]This discussion is largely based on information gained from agents of the FBI Academy, Quantico, Virginia, and from Agent Thomas Strents, who conducted a hostage negotiation program at the Greater St. Louis Police Academy, 1982.

to life's stress and pain is suicide-murder, usually of family members. There is also the phenomenon of the severely deranged person who firmly believes that he is threatened or persecuted by others and sets out to take revenge upon them for their imagined crimes against him. This situation may easily lead to the taking of hostages to enforce clearly irrational demands. The neurotic is one whose thinking and behavior are governed by uncontrollable anxiety or depression.

If, in fact, stress is the precipitating factor in this type of situation, then logically attempts should be made to reduce stress. The passage of time in itself is usually helpful, coupled with a calm attitude of the negotiator toward the subject. Nothing should be done to increase anxiety, such as a precipitous show of force. It is good to remember that such persons are as delicately balanced as a hair trigger. Those who deal with them should proceed on that assumption.

The character disordered, known as psychopaths or sociopaths, are the most complex and difficult with which to deal. This type is not afraid to commit a crime and will usually show no anxiety while doing so. They are not usually upset or nervous, as are the psychotics.

The studies concerning the sociopath seem to indicate that the sociopathic personality is responsible for an inordinate proportion of crimes. He also makes up a significant percentage of our prison population. If this is true, it is logical to assume that he represents a significant number of those who engage in hostage taking, particularly in the case of the trapped armed robber or the prison rioter.

A basic personality trait of the sociopath is lack of conscience, in fact, lack of all humanity. His only concern is, "Can I get away with it?" Appeals to him must always be couched in terms of what is best for him. He will not hesitate to kill hostages, law enforcement officers, and, in some instances, even himself if such an act is sufficiently dramatic. He is extremely impulsive and unable to delay gratification—so those over whom he has control are in constant danger. Moreover, if the hostage is female, rape becomes a very real possibility.

Although the sociopath is not mentally ill in the traditional sense, he represents a potential bombshell in any hostage situation because of impulsive behavior and lack of concern for others. It has been an axiom in hostage situations that the more time the hostage spends with the abductor, the better the chances for the hostage.

This is because of a type of common bond which appears to grow between the two. If the felon is a sociopath, however, such feelings for the hostage are unlikely to develop. His actions will be based only on opportunity and self-indulgence.

One thing to remember is that a person thought to be a common criminal (that is, simply caught in an act of crime) could be suffering from one of these emotional disturbances, which would make the tactical situation more complex. A disturbing reality is that for the emotionally disturbed the mere sight of the tactical team could trigger a violent reaction.

The emotionally disturbed are those more commonly encountered in the family disturbance.

The last character type (though not necessarily emotionally disturbed) is the terrorist or the radical activist. Such a person may be encountered individually or in a group. They are driven by ideals that dominate their thoughts and actions. Tactical situations they might create are usually for the purpose of bringing attention to their cause or ideals. They will at times carry their ideals to the point of total destruction of not only themselves but to everyone involved, including hostages and police.

These groups are often well-equipped and heavily armed and sometimes trained in urban guerrilla warfare. Therefore, they should be considered uncontrollable by a small tactical team. Such a team should, if possible, wait for the assistance of other departments or for that of federal authorities.

Situations created by these groups are usually well planned and sometimes even rehearsed. They would probably be knowledgeable of tactical procedures and would therefore be ready with countermoves. This is one way in which they attempt to discredit the authorities and to make the police appear foolish or unprofessional in the eyes of the public and news media. These groups often claim responsibility (and may be responsible) for many of today's ambush attacks on police, sniping incidents, and bombings of public and administrative buildings.

Fortunately, these groups are not commonly confronted by local police agencies, and when this does occur, the local agencies are usually working hand-in-hand with federal authorities.

Appendix B
Hand Signals

This hand signal method section has been designed to assist officers in communicating when verbal or radio communications are unavailable or possibly not practical. This hand signal style has been designed keeping simplicity in mind, and with a little practice, all team members should be able to perform them with little effort and still be understood.

Knowing the amount of mental pressure officers will be under during a tactical situation, these signals should be practiced whenever possible during training. This will allow hand signaling to come as a reflex rather than having to stop and spend time thinking about signals when the extra time may not be available.

Order—Hold the forearm in a vertical position with a clinched fist. This indicates a firm order.

Go—Swing the arm and hand from the rear forward, indicating to move forward or go.

Message Received—Hold the arm outstretched, forming a circle with the index finger and thumb toward the receiving officer.

Come—Hold the arm outstretched and, bending at the elbow, draw your hand toward your own body.

Don't Understand or Unknown—Bend your elbows with the palms of your hands facing up.

No—Rotate the head from side to side.

Yes—Rotate the head up and down.

Me or Myself—Point your index finger at your own chest.

See—Hold the hand in a parallel position over the eyes.

Hear—Hold the hand behind the ear with the palm of the hand facing the receiving officer.

You—Hold the arm outstretched and point the index finger at the receiving officer.

Stop—Hold the arm outstretched with the palm of the hand facing the receiving officer.

Understood—Bending your elbow, raise your arm and clench your fist with the palm of your hand facing the receiving officer.

Disregard Last Signal—Raise your open hand to your chest, then move the hand from side to side.

Numbers—Can be indicated by holding up the proper number of fingers.

There—Point the index finger with the arm outstretched to the object or location indicated.

Armed—Outstretch your arm toward the receiving officer, bend your wrist, and form a pistol shape with your fingers.

Door or Doorway—Form the shape of a door or rectangle without closing the bottom.

Window—Follow the same shape as a doorway but finish by bringing your fingers together to close the triangle.

Car or Vehicle—Clench your fists and form a circle in front of your body as if turning a steering wheel.

Commander or Field Supervisor—Reach across your body and place three fingers on your other sleeve.

Suspect—Reach across your body and take hold of the wrist of your other arm.

Adult or Tall—Hold outstretched arm high with palm facing down.

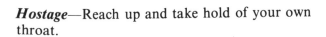

Hostage—Reach up and take hold of your own throat.

Juvenile—Hold your outstretched arm in a low position with the palm of your hand facing down.